NYC GUITAR SCHOOL SONGS FOR BEGINNERS

ALL OF ME: JOHN LEGEND • ANYONE ELSE BUT YOU: THE MOLDY PEACHES • BAD MOON RISING: CREEDENCE CLEARWATER REVIVAL • BEST DAY OF MY LIFE: AMERICAN AUTHORS • BREAKFAST AT TIFFANY'S: DEEP BLUE SOMETHING • BROWN EYED GIRL: VAN MORRISON • COME AS YOU ARE: NIRVANA • DESPACITO: LUIS FONSI & DADDY YANKEE FEAT. JUSTIN BIEBER • DON'T YOU (FORGET ABOUT ME): SIMPLE MINDS • FIGHT SONG: RACHEL PLATTEN • GIVE PEACE A CHANCE: PLASTIC ONO BAND • I'M YOURS: JASON MRAZ • JOLENE: DOLLY PARTON • KNOCKIN' ON HEAVEN'S DOOR: BOB DYLAN • LAST KISS: PEARL JAM • LET IT GO: JAMES BAY • MAD WORLD: TEARS FOR FEARS • MAN ON THE MOON: R.E.M. • MY NAME IS JONAS: WEEZER • NO RAIN: BLIND MELON • THE ONLY EXCEPTION: PARAMORE • PERFECT: ED SHEERAN • SHAKE IT OFF: TAYLOR SWIFT • SWEET CHILD O' MINE: GUNS N' ROSES • TICKET TO RIDE: THE BEATLES • TWIST AND SHOUT: THE BEATLES • VIVA LA VIDA: COLDPLAY • WE ARE YOUNG: FUN. FEATURING JANELLE MONAE • WE'RE GOING TO BE FRIENDS: THE WHITE STRIPES • WHAT I GOT: SUBLIME • WONDERWALL: OASIS • ZOMBIE: THE CRANBERRIES

Arrangements by Rob Alder

Edited by Dan Emery

ISBN 978-1-5400-4238-5

HAL•LEONARD®

Visit Hal Leonard Online at
www.halleonard.com

Contact us:
Hal Leonard
7777 West Bluemound Road
Milwaukee, WI 53213
Email: info@halleonard.com

In Europe, contact:
Hal Leonard Europe Limited
42 Wigmore Street
Marylebone, London, W1U 2RN
Email: info@halleonardeurope.com

In Australia, contact:
Hal Leonard Australia Pty. Ltd.
4 Lentara Court
Cheltenham, Victoria, 3192 Australia
Email: info@halleonard.com.au

INTRODUCTION

To be a guitar player, you must play guitar—it's that simple! But the problem is that for those who are just beginning their guitar journey, the excitement of learning a first chord or strum can quickly give way to discouragement.

In fact, according to a recent study from liveforlivemusic.com, *90% of new guitar players quit playing within a year after purchasing their first guitar!*

What a heartbreaking statistic! That's thousands of people who want to play guitar because they love music, want to express themselves, connect with others, play for family and friends, write or perform music, or simply enjoy learning a new skill, who **failed**.

That's where **this book** comes in! This book can literally be the difference between being one of the 10% who stick with playing guitar instead of joining the sad majority who regretfully set their guitar dreams aside.

You see, as the founder of one of America's largest guitar schools and after three decades of teaching guitar, I can tell you that the secret to success in guitar is simple: It's setting yourself up for success in the first place!

People fail at learning guitar when they don't have a **structure** to keep them **on track** with step-by-step increases in difficulty to make learning easy and fun.

That's what this book provides—a **step-by-step** and **song-by-song** method to ensure that even absolute beginners can play.

If you're looking for a songbook with advanced note-for-note transcriptions of songs, this isn't it! These arrangements are *super simple*, based on the revolutionary NYC Guitar School: Guitar for Absolute Beginners book and method used by over 15,000 busy New Yorkers to successfully learn to play guitar. These step-by-step chord progressions and simple strumming patterns are matched with dozens of great songs from the incredible Hal Leonard catalog of songs. The result is a motivating and inviting book that even a beginner can pick up and make music with.

The book can be used as a companion to the NYC Guitar School course (**visit www.nycguitarschool.com/hl** for free downloads and resources) or students and teachers can use it as a stand alone, song-by-song method for beginning to learn guitar.

I am so thrilled that Hal Leonard has partnered with New York City Guitar School to allow us to bring this book of super simple songs for Absolute Beginners to you, and I'm also thrilled that you have picked it up!

There's a difference between dreaming and being. And that difference is doing.

If you're serious about playing guitar, it is easier than you think. And this little book can be your trusty guide and companion.

So what are you waiting for? On to guitar, and on to greatness! I know you won't regret it.

Dan Emery

Dan Emery
Founder, NYC Guitar School

NOTE

This songbook is a wonderful companion to the New York City Guitar School: Guitar for Absolute Beginners course, which is a highly effective step-by-step method to go from absolute ignorance in guitar to playing full songs with confidence.

WEEK 1: Parts of the guitar, rest strokes, fretting, D, chord diagrams, G, plant fingers and practice tips.

WEEK 2 Tuning, playing with a pick, quarter note strums, A7, tablature and how to memorize songs.

WEEK 3: G, Em, C, D7 and pivot fingers.

WEEK 4: Alternate strumming and small barres.

WEEK 5 Riffs, Am, and G to C direct changes.

WEEK 6 The "Basic Strum"—your introduction to mixing down and up strums.

WEEK 7: The "Best Strum"—the most important and commonly used strum pattern in guitar.

WEEK 8: A, E, and an introduction to basic chord theory.

WEEK 9: Mixed rhythms and split measures.

WEEK 10: Week 10 show!

CONTENTS

What I Got

Performed by Sublime

Arranged by NYC Guitar School

Words and Music by Brad Nowell, Eric Wilson,
Floyd Gaugh and Lindon Roberts

D   G   C

Intro

① 2 ③ 4 | ① 2 ③ 4

D **G** | **D** **G** |

Verse 1

① 2 ③ 4 | ① 2 ③ 4

D **G** | **D** **G** |

Ear - ly in the morn - in', ris - in' to the street.

① 2 ③ 4 | ① 2 ③ 4

D **G** | **D** **G** |

Light me up that cig - a - rette and I strap shoes on my feet.

① 2 ③ 4 | ① 2 ③ 4

D **G** | **D** **G** |

Got to find a rea - son, rea - son things went wrong.

① 2 ③ 4 | ① 2 ③ 4

D **G** | **D** **G** |

Got to find a rea - son why my mon - ey's all gone.

① 2 ③ 4 | ① 2 ③ 4

D **G** | **D** **G** |

I got a Dal - ma - tion, and I can still get high.

① 2 ③ 4 | ① 2 ③ 4

D **G** | **D** **G** |

I can play the gui - tar like a moth - er - f**k - in' ri - ot.

Interlude

① 2 ③ 4 | ① 2 ③ 4

‖: **D** **G** | **D** **G** :‖

(2nd time) Well, life

% **Verse 2 & 3**

⊓   ⊓   ⊓   ⊓
①   2   ③   4   ①   2   ③   4

D   **G**   **D**   **G**

is too short so love the one you got 'cause you might get run o - ver or you might get shot.
Why, I don't cry when my dog runs a - way. I don't get an-gry at the bills I have to pay.

① 2 ③ 4 ① 2 ③ 4

D   **G**   **D**   **G**

Nev - er start no stat - ic, I just get it off my chest. Nev - er had to bat - tle with no bul - et - proof vest.
I don't get an - gry when my mom smokes pot, hits the bot - tle and moves right to the rock.

① 2 ③ 4 ① 2 ③ 4

D   **G**   **D**   **G**

Take a small ex - am - ple, take a ti-ti-ti - tip from me, Take all of your mon - ey, give it all to char - i - ty. Love
F**k-in' and fight-in', it's all the same. Liv' - in' with Lou - ie Dog's the on - ly way to stay sane.

To Coda ⊕

① 2 ③ 4 ① 2 ③ 4

D   **G**   **D**   **G**

is what I got, it's with - in my reach and the Sub - lime style's still straight from Long Beach. It all comes
Let the lov - in', let the lov - in' come back

① 2 ③ 4 ① 2 ③ 4

D   **G**   **D**   **G**

back to you, you fi - na'ly get what you de - serve. Try and test that, you're bound to get served.

① 2 ③ 4 ① 2 ③ 4

D   **G**   **D**   **G**

Love's what I got, don't start a ri - ot. You feel it when the dance gets hot.

① 2 ③ 4 ① 2 ③ 4

D   **G**   **D**   **G**

Lov - in' is what I got. I said re - mem - ber that.

Chorus

① 2 ③ 4 ① 2 ③ 4

D   **G** | **D**   **G**

Lov - in'   is what I   got.   and re - mem - ber that.

① 2 ③ 4 ① 2 ③ 4

D   **G** | **D**   **G**

Lov - in'   is what I   got,   I said re - mem - ber that.

D.S. al Coda

① 2 ③ 4 ① 2 ③ 4

D   **G** | **D**   **G**

Lov - in'   is what I   got,   I   got,   I   got, I   got.

⊕ Interlude

① 2 ③ ④ ① 2 ③ ④ ① 2 ③ ④ ① 2 ③ 4 ① 2 ③ 4

D   ‖: **D**   **C**   **G** | **D**   **C**   **G** :‖ **D**

to me.   'Cause

Outro

① 2 ③ ④ ① 2 ③ ④ ① 2 ③ ④

     C   **G** | **D**   **C**   **G** | **D**   **C**   **G**

lov - in'   is what I   got.   I said re - mem - ber that.   Lov - in'   is what I

① 2 ③ ④ ① 2 ③ ④

D   **C**   **G** | **D**   **C**   **G**

got,   and re - mem - ber that.   Lov - in'   is what I

① 2 ③ ④ ① 2 ③ ④

D   **C**   **G** | **D**   **C**   **G**

got.   I said re - mem - ber that.   Lov - in'   is what I

① 2 ③ ④ ① 2 ③ 4 ① 2 ③ 4 ① 2 3 4

D   **G** | **D**   **G** | **D**   **G** | **D**

got, I got, I got, I got.

Anyone Else But You

from the Motion Picture soundtrack JUNO

Performed by The Moldy Peaches
Arranged by NYC Guitar School

Words and Music by
Kimya Dawson and Adam Green

D G

Intro

D | G |

D | G | You're a

Verse 1 & 2

:D | G |

part - time lover and a full time friend. The monkey on your back is the lat - est trend. I
kiss you on the brain in the shadow of the train. I kiss you all starry eyed, my body's swinging from side to side. I

D | G |

don't see what any - one can see in any - one else but you. I
don't see what any - one can see in any - one else but you.

Verse 3 & 4

:D | G |

Here is the church and here is the steeple. We sure are cute for two ugly people. I
pebbles for - give me, the trees for - give me. So why can't you for - give me? I

D | G |

don't see what any - one can see in any - one else but you. The
don't see what any - one can see in any - one else but you.

Verse 5 & Interlude

:D | G |

I will find my niche in your car with my M - P - 3, D - V - D, rumble packed gui - tar. I
Do do do do do do do do do do do. Do do do do do do do do do do do do.

D | G |

don't see what any - one can see in any - one else but you.
Do do do do do do do do do do do do do.

Verse 6 & 7

||: D |G

Up, up, down, down, left, right, left, right, B, A, Start. Just be - cause we use cheats doesn't mean we're not smart.   I
You   are   always   trying to keep   it   real.   I'm   in   love with   how   you   feel.   I

D |G   :||

don't   see what any - one can see   in any - one   else   but   you.
don't   see what any - one can see   in any - one   else   but   you. We

Verse 8 & 9

||: D |G

both   have   shiny   happy   fits   of   rage.   You   want   more   fans.   I   want   more   stage.   I
Don   Qui - xote   was a   steel - driving   man.   My   name   is   Adam; I'm your   big - gest   fan.   I

D |G   :||

don't   see what any - one can see   in any - one   else   but   you.
don't   see what any - one can see   in any - one   else   but   you.

Verse 10

D |G

Squinched - up your face   and   did   a   dance.   Shook a little   turd out of the   bottom   of your pants.   I

D |G

don't   see what any - one can see   in any - one   else   but   you.

Outro

D |G

Do   do do do   do do   do   do do do do.   Do   do do do   do do   do   do do do do.

D |G ||

Do   do do do   do do   do   do do do do   do   but   you.

Best Day of My Life

Performed by American Authors
Arranged by NYC Guitar School

Words and Music by
Zachary Barnett, James Adam Shelley,
Matthew Sanchez, David Rublin,
Shep Goodman and Aaron Accetta

D G

Intro

D | G |

Woo, woo, woo. I

Verse 1

D | G |

had a dream so big and loud, I jumped so high, I touched the clouds. Whoa oh oh oh oh oh oh. (Whoa oh oh oh oh oh.) I

D | G |

stretched my hands out to the sky, we danced with mon-sters through the night. Whoa oh oh oh oh oh. (Whoa oh oh oh oh oh.) I'm

D | G |

nev-er gon-na look back, whoa. I'm nev-er gon-na give it up, no. Please don't wake me now. (Two, three, four.)

Chorus

D | G |

Woo, woo, woo. This is gon-na be the best day of my life. My li - i - i - i - i - ife.

D | G |

Woo, woo, woo. This is gon-na be the best day of my life. My li - i - i - i - i - ife.

D | G |

Woo, woo, woo. Woo, woo, woo. I

Verse 2

D | G |

how-led at the moon with friends and then the sun came crash-ing in. Whoa oh oh oh oh oh oh. (Whoa oh oh oh oh oh.) But

D | G |

all the pos-si-bil - i - ties, no lim-its just e - piph - a - nies. Whoa oh oh oh oh oh. (Whoa oh oh oh oh oh.) I'm

D | |G | |

nev-er gon-na look back, whoa. I'm nev-er gon-na give it up, no. Just don't wake me now.

Chorus

D | |G | |

Woo, woo, woo. This is gon-na be the best day of my life. My li - i - i - i - i - ife.

D | |G | |

Woo, woo, woo. This is gon-na be the best day of my life. My li - i - i - i - i - ife.

D | |G | |

Woo, woo, woo. Woo, woo, woo.

Bridge

D | | |

I hear it call - ing out-side my win - dow, I feel it in my soul, soul. The

D | | |

The stars were burn-ing so bright, the sun was out 'til mid - night. I say we lose con - trol. con - trol.

D | |G | |

Woo, woo, woo. I

Outro

‖: D | |G | :‖

Woo, woo, woo. This is gon-na be the best day of my life. My li - i - i - i - i - ife.

D | |G | |

This is gon-na be, this is gon-na be, this is gon-na be the best day of my life. Ev-'ry-thing is look-ing up, ev'ry-bod-y up now.

D | |G | |D ‖

Woo, woo, woo. This is gon-na be the best day of my life. My li - i - i - i - i - ife.

Capo VI

Give Peace a Chance

Performed by The Plastic Ono Band
Arranged by NYC Guitar School

Words and Music by
John Lennon

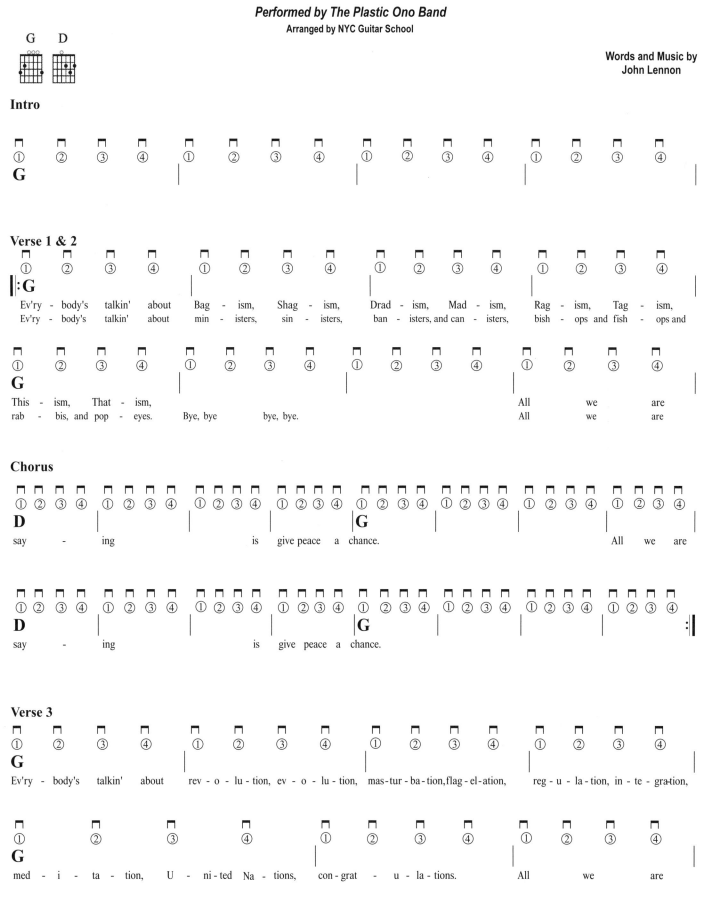

Chorus

D ... G
say - ing is give peace a chance. All we are

D ... G
say - ing is give peace a chance.

Verse 4

G
Ev'ry - body's talkin' about John and Yo - ko, Tim - my Lear - y Rose mar - y. Tom - my Smoth - ers, Bob - by Dyl - an, Tom - my Coop - er,

G
Der - ek Tay - lor, Nor - man Mail - er, Al - an Gins - berg, Har - e Kris - na Har - e, Har - e Kris - na. All we are

Chorus

D ... G
say - ing is give peace a chance. All we are

D ... G
say - ing is give peace a chance.

Outro

G |: D
All we are say - ing is give peace a

1.-11. | 12.

G :|
chance. All we are

Bad Moon Rising

Performed by Creedence Clearwater Revival
Arranged by NYC Guitar School

Words and Music by
John Fogerty

D   A7   G

Intro

⊓ ⊓ ⊓ ⊓ ⊓ ⊓ ⊓ ⊓ ⊓ ⊓ ⊓ ⊓ ⊓ ⊓ ⊓ ⊓
① + ② + ③ + ④ + ① + ② + ③ + ④ + ① + ② + ③ + ④ + ① + ② + ③ + ④ +

D |**A7**   **G** |**D** |

Verse

⊓ ⊓ ⊓ ⊓ ⊓ ⊓ ⊓ ⊓ ⊓ ⊓ ⊓ ⊓ ⊓ ⊓ ⊓ ⊓
① + ② + ③ + ④ + ① + ② + ③ + ④ + ① + ② + ③ + ④ + ① + ② + ③ + ④ +

‖: **D** |**A7**   **G** |**D** |

I   see   a   bad   moon   a ris - in'.
I   hear   hur - ri - canes   a blow - in'.

⊓ ⊓ ⊓ ⊓ ⊓ ⊓ ⊓ ⊓ ⊓ ⊓ ⊓ ⊓ ⊓ ⊓ ⊓ ⊓
① + ② + ③ + ④ + ① + ② + ③ + ④ + ① + ② + ③ + ④ + ① + ② + ③ + ④ +

D |**A7**   **G** |**D** |

I   see   trou - ble   on   the   way.
I   know   the   end   is   com - ing soon.

⊓ ⊓ ⊓ ⊓ ⊓ ⊓ ⊓ ⊓ ⊓ ⊓ ⊓ ⊓ ⊓ ⊓ ⊓ ⊓
① + ② + ③ + ④ + ① + ② + ③ + ④ + ① + ② + ③ + ④ + ① + ② + ③ + ④ +

D |**A7**   **G** |**D** |

I   see   earth - quakes and light - nin'.
I   fear   riv - ers   o - ver - flow - in'.

⊓ ⊓ ⊓ ⊓ ⊓ ⊓ ⊓ ⊓ ⊓ ⊓ ⊓ ⊓ ⊓ ⊓ ⊓ ⊓
① + ② + ③ + ④ + ① + ② + ③ + ④ + ① + ② + ③ + ④ + ① + ② + ③ + ④ +

D |**A7**   **G** |**D** |

I   see   bad   times   to - day. ⎫
I   hear   the   voice   of   rage   and ruin. ⎭

Chorus

⊓ ⊓ ⊓ ⊓ ⊓ ⊓ ⊓ ⊓ ⊓ ⊓ ⊓ ⊓ ⊓ ⊓ ⊓ ⊓
① + ② + ③ + ④ + ① + ② + ③ + ④ + ① + ② + ③ + ④ + ① + ② + ③ + ④ +

G | |**D** |

Don't   go a - round to - night.   Well, it's   bound   to   take   your   life.

⊓ ⊓ ⊓ ⊓ ⊓ ⊓ ⊓ ⊓ ⊓ ⊓ ⊓ ⊓ ⊓ ⊓ ⊓ ⊓
① + ② + ③ + ④ + ① + ② + ③ + ④ + ① + ② + ③ + ④ + ① + ② + ③ + ④ +

A7 |**G**   **D** | :‖

There's   a   bad   moon   on   the   rise.

Guitar Solo

‖:D |A7   G |D | :‖

G | |D |

A7 |G |D |

Verse 3

D |A7   G |D |

Hope you   got   your   things to - geth   -   er.

D |A7   G |D |

Hope you   are   quite pre   -   pared   to die.

D |A7   G |D |

Looks   like   we're   in   for   nas - ty weath   -   er.

D |A7   G |D |

One   eye   is   tak - en   for   an eye.   Well,

Chorus

‖:G | |D |

don't   go a-round to-night.   Well, it's bound to take your life.

A7 |G |D   :‖

There's   a bad   moon   on   the rise.

Twist and Shout

Performed by The Beatles
Arranged by NYC Guitar School

Words and Music by
Bert Russell and Phil Medley

D   G   A7

Intro

D   G |A7 |D   G |A7 |

Well, shake it up, ba-

Chorus

D   G |A7 |D   G |A7 |

– by, now. (Shake it up, ba - by.)   twist   and   shout.   (Twist and shout.)   Come on, come on, come on, come on,

D   G |A7 |D   G |A7 |

ba - by,   now.   Come on and work it on out.   (Work it on out.)   Well, work it on out.

Verse 1

D   G |A7 |D   G |A7 |

(Work it on out.)   You know you look   so   good.   (Look so   good.)   You know you got   me

D   G |A7 |D   G |A7 |

go - in' now. (Got me go - in'.)   Just like I knew   you would.   (Like I knew   you would.)   Well, shake it up, ba-

Chorus

D   G |A7 |D   G |A7 |

– by, now. (Shake it up, ba - by.)   twist   and   shout.   (Twist and shout.)   Come on, come on, come on, come on,

D   G |A7 |D   G |A7 |

ba - by,   now.   Come on and work it on out.   (Work it on out.)   You know you twist, it little   girl.

Verse 2

D   G |A7 |D   G |A7 |

_____   (Twist, lit - tle girl.)   You know you twist   so   fine.   (Twist so   fine.)   Come on   and   twist lit - tle

⊓ ① ⊓ ② ⊓ ③ ⊓ ④ ⊓ ① ⊓ ② ⊓ ③ ⊓ ④ ⊓ ① ⊓ ② ⊓ ③ ⊓ ④ ⊓ ① ⊓ ② ⊓ ③ ⊓ ④

D　　　**G**　　|**A7**　　　　|**D**　　　**G**　　|**A7**　　　　　|

clo - ser　now. (Twist a little clo - ser.) And let me know　that you're　mine.　(Let me know　you're mine.)

Interlude

D　　　**G**　　|**A7**　　　　|**D**　　　**G**　　|**A7**　　　　　|

A7　　　|　　|　　|　　|　　|

Ah, ————— ah, ————ah, ——————— ah, ——————ah. ———————Wow!　Well, shake it　up, ba -

Chorus

D　　　**G**　　|**A7**　　　　|**D**　　　**G**　　|**A7**　　　　　|

- by now, (Shake it up, ba - by.)　Twist　　and　　shout.　(Twist and shout.)　Come on, come on, come on, come on,

D　　　**G**　　|**A7**　　　　|**D**　　　**G**　　|**A7**　　　　　|

ba - by,　now.　Come on and work it on out.　(Work it on out.)　You know you twist it, little girl.

Verse 3

D　　　**G**　　|**A7**　　　　|**D**　　　**G**　　|**A7**　　　　　|

(Twist, lit - tle girl.)　You know you twist　so　fine.　(Twist so　fine.)　Come on and twist a lit - tle

D　　　**G**　　|**A7**　　　　|**D**　　　**G**　　|**A7**　　　　　|

clo - ser　now. (Twist a little clo - ser.) And let me know　that you're　mine. (Let me know　you're mine.)　Well, shake it, shake it, shake it,

Outro

D　　　**G**　　|**A7**　　　　|**D**　　　**G**　　|**A7**　　　　　|

ba - by,　now. (Shake it　up, ba - by.) Well, shake it, shake it, shake it,　ba - by,　now. (Shake it up, ba by.) Well, shake it, shake it, shake it,

D　　　**G**　　|**A7**　　|　　|

ba - by,　now. (Shake it　up, ba - by.)　Ah, ——————————— ah, ———————————

⊓ ① ⊓ ② ⊓ ③ ⊓ ④ ⊓ ① ⊓ ② ⊓ ③ ⊓ ④ ⊓ ① ⊓ ② ⊓ ③ ⊓ ④ ⊓ ① 2　3　4

|　　|　　|**D**　　　||

ah, ——————— ah, ——————— ah, ———————

Breakfast at Tiffany's

Performed by Deep Blue Something
Arranged by NYC Guitar School

Words and Music by
Todd Pipes

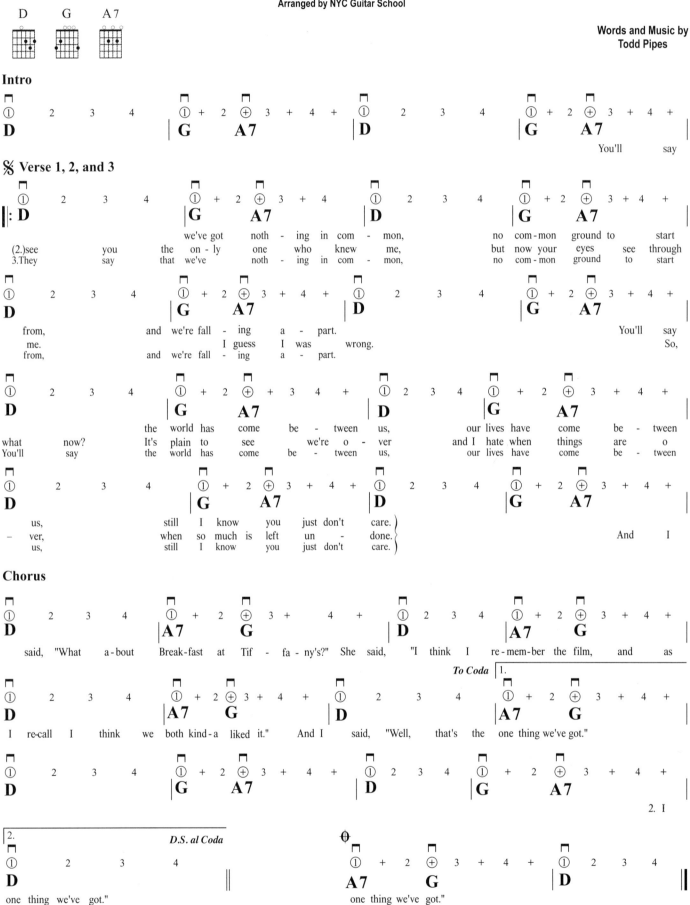

Perfect

Performed by Ed Sheeran
Arranged by NYC Guitar School

Word and Music by
Ed Sheeran

G   Em   C   D

Verse 1

③ ④ ① ② ③ ④ ① ② ③ ④

G I found a love   for   me. **Em**   Dar-ling, just

① ② ③ ④ ① ② ③ ④

C dive   right in,   fol - low my **D** lead.   Well, I found a girl,

① ② ③ ④ ① ② ③ ④

G   beau - ti - ful and sweet. **Em**   Well, I nev - er

① ② ③ ④ ① ② ③ ④

C knew you were the some - one wait-ing for **D** me.   'Cause we were just kids when we

𝄋 Pre-Chorus

① ② ③ ④ ① ② ③ ④

G fell   in   love,   not know-ing **Em** what   it   was.   I   will not
    so   in   love,   fight - ing a - gainst all   odds   I   know we'll

① ② ③ ④ ① ② ③ ④

C give   you   up   this **G** time.   **D**   Dar - ling, just
    be   all   right this this time.   Dar - ling, just

① ② ③ ④ ① ② ③ ④

G kiss   me   slow,   your heart is **Em** all   I   own.   And in   your
    hold   my   hand. Be my girl, I'll be   your   man.   I   see   my

① ② ③ ④ ① ② ③ ④

C eyes,   you're hold - ing mine. }
    fu - ture   in   your eyes. } **D**   Ba - by,

Chorus

Em   **C** | **G**   **D**
I'm   danc - ing in the   dark   with you be - tween my

Em   **C** | **G**   **D**
arms.   Bare - foot on the   grass,   lis - ten - ing to   our

Em   **C** | **G**   **D**
fa - v'rite song. When you   said   you looked   a   mess,   I   whis - pered   un - der - neath   my
When   I   saw   you in   that   dress,   look - ing so   beau - ti - ful,   I

To Coda ⊕

Em   **C** | **G**   **D**
breath, but you   heard   it,   "Dar - ling,"   you   look   per - fect to - night.
don't   de - serve   this.   "Dar - ling,

Interlude

G   **D**   **Em**   **D** | **C**   **D**
               Well, I   found a

Verse 2

G |**Em**
wom - an,   strong - er than an - y - one I   know.   She shares my

C |**D**
dreams,   I   hope   that some - day,   I'll share her   home.   I   found a love

G |**Em**
     to   car - ry   more   than just   my se - crets,   to car - ry

D.S. al Coda

C |**D**
love,   to car - ry chil - dren   of our   own.   We are still kids, but we're

φ

① ② ③ ④

G   **D**

you   look   per   -   fect   to - night.

Solo

① ② ③ ④   ① ② ③ ④   ① ② ③ ④   ① ② ③ ④

G |**Em**   **C** |**D**

                            Ba - by,

Chorus

① ② ③ ④ ① ② ③ ④

Em   **C** |**G**   **D**

I'm   danc - ing   in   the   dark   with   you   be - tween   my

① ② ③ ④ ① ② ③ ④

Em   **C** |**G**   **D**

arms.   Bare - foot   on   the   grass,   lis - ten - ing   to   our

① ② ③ ④ ① ② ③ ④

Em   **C** |**G**   **D**

fa - v'rite song.   I   have faith   in   what   I   see,   now   I   know   I   have met   an

① ② ③ ④ ① ② ③ ④

Em   **C** |**G**   **D**

an - gel   in   per - son   and   she   looks   per - fect.   I

① ② ③ ④ ① ② ③ ④

C |**D**

don't   de   -   serve   this,   you   look   per - fect   to-night.

Outro

① ② ③ ④ ① ② ③ ④ ①   2   3   4

G **D** **Em** **D** |**C**   **D** |**G**

Last Kiss

Performed by Pearl Jam
Arranged by NYC Guitar School

Words and Music by
Wayne Cochran

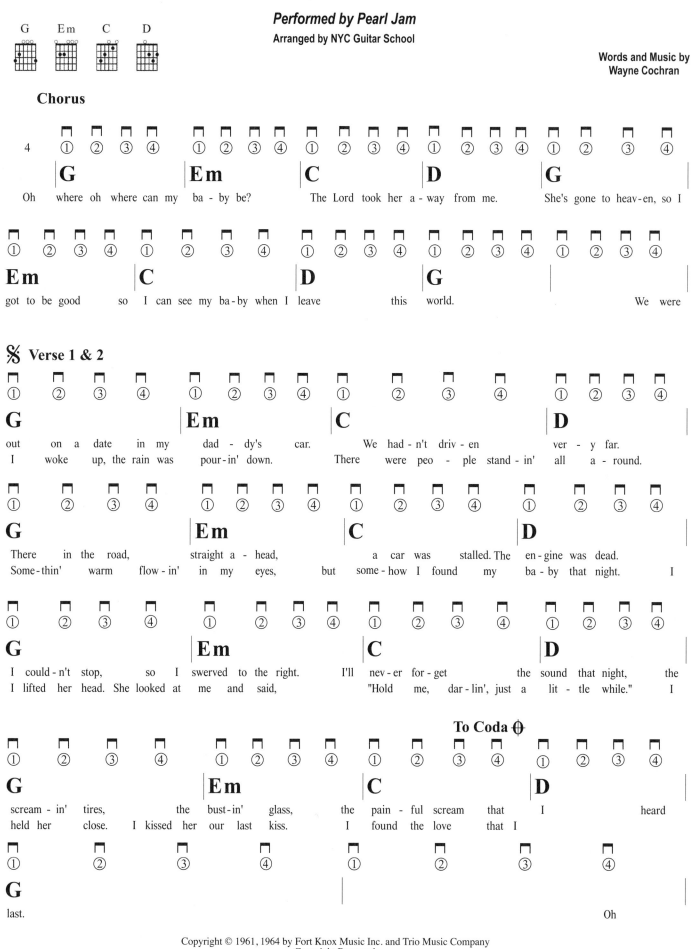

Chorus

⊓① ⊓② ⊓③ ⊓④ ⊓① ⊓② ⊓③ ⊓④ ⊓① ⊓② ⊓③ ⊓④ ⊓① ⊓② ⊓③ ⊓④

G |**Em** |**C** |**D**

where, oh where, can my ba - by be? The Lord took her a - way from me.

⊓① ⊓② ⊓③ ⊓④ ⊓① ⊓② ⊓③ ⊓④ ⊓① ⊓② ⊓③ ⊓④ ⊓① ⊓② ⊓③ ⊓④

G |**Em** |**C** |**D** |

She's gone to heav - en, so I got to be good so I can see my ba - by when I leave this

D.S. al Coda

⊓① ⊓② ⊓③ ⊓④ ⊓① ⊓② ⊓③ ⊓④

G | |

world. When

Coda

⊓① ⊓② ⊓③ ⊓④ ⊓① ⊓② ⊓③ ⊓④ ⊓① ⊓② ⊓③ ⊓④ ⊓① ⊓② ⊓③ ⊓④

D |**G** |**Em** |**C** |

knew I'd miss. Well, now she's gone e - ven though I hold her tight. I lost my love my

⊓① ⊓② ⊓③ ⊓④ ⊓① ⊓② ⊓③ ⊓④ ⊓① ⊓② ⊓③ ⊓④

D |**G** |

life that night. Oh

Chorus

⊓① ⊓② ⊓③ ⊓④ ⊓① ⊓② ⊓③ ⊓④ ⊓① ⊓② ⊓③ ⊓④ ⊓① ⊓② ⊓③ ⊓④

G |**Em** |**C** |**D** |

where, oh where, can my ba - by be? The Lord took her a - way from me.

⊓① ⊓② ⊓③ ⊓④ ⊓① ⊓② ⊓③ ⊓④ ⊓① ⊓② ⊓③ ⊓④ ⊓① ⊓② ⊓③ ⊓④

G |**Em** |**C** |**D** |

She's gone to heav - en, so I got to be good so I can see my ba - by when I leave this

⊓① ⊓② ⊓③ ⊓④ ⊓① ⊓② ⊓③ ⊓④

G | |

world.

Outro

⊓① ⊓② ⊓③ ⊓④ ⊓① ⊓② ⊓③ ⊓④ ⊓① ⊓② ⊓③ ⊓④ ⊓① ⊓② ⊓③ ⊓④

|: **G** |**Em** |**C** |**D** |

⊓① ⊓② ⊓③ ⊓④ ⊓① ⊓② ⊓③ ⊓④ ⊓① ⊓② ⊓③ ⊓④ ⊓① ② 3 4

G |**Em** |**C** |**D** :|**G** |

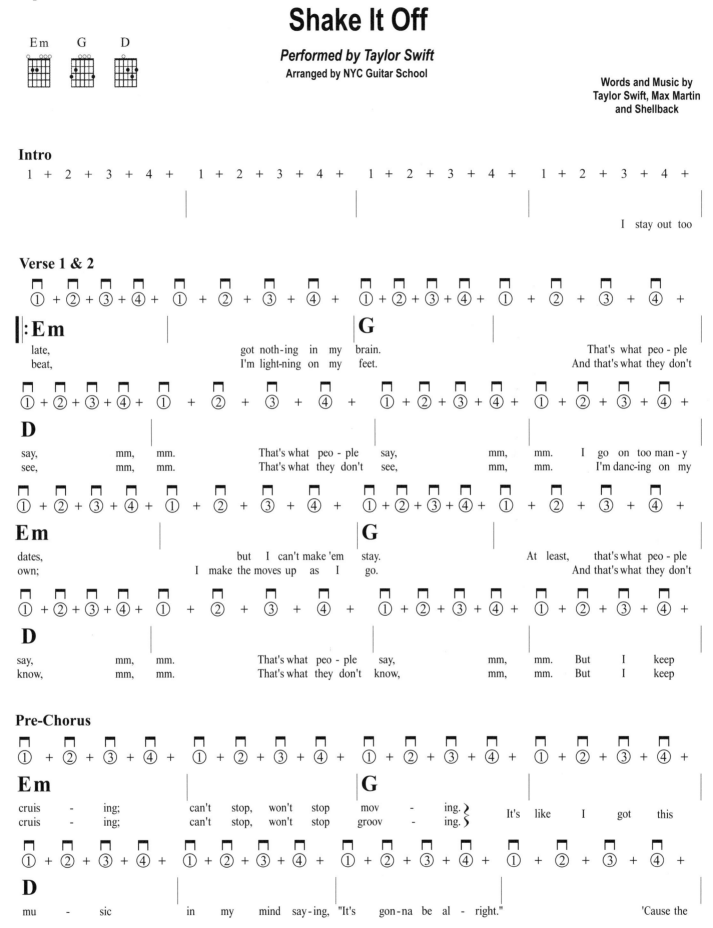

Chorus

∏ ∏ ∏ ∏ | ∏ ∏ ∏ ∏ | ∏ ∏ ∏ ∏ | ∏ ∏ ∏ ∏
① + ② + ③ + ④ + ① + ② + ③ + ④ + ① + ② + ③ + ④ + ① + ② + ③ + ④ +

Em | | **G** | |

play-ers gon-na play, play, play, play, play, and the hat-ers gon-na hate, hate, hate, hate, hate, ba - by.

∏ ∏ ∏ ∏ | ∏ ∏ ∏ ∏ | ∏ ∏ ∏ ∏ | ∏ ∏ ∏ ∏
① + ② + ③ + ④ + ① + ② + ③ + ④ + ① + ② + ③ + ④ + ① + ② + ③ + ④ +

D | | | |

I'm just gon-na shake, shake, shake, shake, shake; I shake it off, I shake it off. Heart-

∏ ∏ ∏ ∏ | ∏ ∏ ∏ ∏ | ∏ ∏ ∏ ∏ | ∏ ∏ ∏ ∏
① + ② + ③ + ④ + ① + ② + ③ + ④ + ① + ② + ③ + ④ + ① + ② + ③ + ④ +

Em | | **G** | |

break-ers gon-na break, break, break, break, break and the fak-ers gon-na fake, fake, fake, fake, fake, ba - by.

1.

∏ ∏ ∏ ∏ | ∏ ∏ ∏ ∏ | ∏ ∏ ∏ ∏ | ∏ ∏ ∏ ∏
① + ② + ③ + ④ + ① + ② + ③ + ④ + ① + ② + ③ + ④ + ① + ② + ③ + ④ +

D | | | :||

I'm just gon-na shake, shake, shake, shake, shake; I shake it off, I shake it off. I nev-er miss a

2.

∏ ∏ ∏ ∏ | ∏ ∏ ∏ ∏ | ∏ ∏ ∏ ∏ | ∏ ∏ ∏ ∏ | ∏ ∏ ∏ ∏
①+②+③+④+ ① + ② + ③ + ④ + ①+②+③+④+ ① + ② + ③ + ④ + ①+②+③+④+

D |**Em** | | **G** | |

off. I shake it off, I shake it off. I, I, I shake it off, I shake it off. I, I, I

∏ ∏ ∏ ∏ | ∏ ∏ ∏ ∏ | ∏ ∏ ∏ ∏ | ∏ ∏ ∏ ∏
① + ② + ③ + ④ + ① + ② + ③ + ④ + ① + ② + ③ + ④ + ① + ② + ③ + ④ +

D | | | |

shake it off, I shake it off. I, I, I shake it off, I shake it off.

Bridge

1 + 2 + 3 + 4 + 1 + 2 + 3 + 4 + 1 + 2 + 3 + 4 + 1 + 2 + 3 + 4 +

||: **N.C.** | | | |

Hey, hey, hey! Just think: While you've been gettin' down and out about the liars
My ex - man brought his new girl - friend. She's like "Oh, my god!" I'm just gon-na shake. And to the

1 + 2 + 3 + 4 + 1 + 2 + 3 + 4 + 1 + 2 + 3 + 4 + 1 + 2 + 3 + 4 +

| | | :||

and the dirty dirty cheats of the world, you could've been gettin' down to this sick beat.
fell - a o - ver there with the hell a good hair, won't you come on o-ver ba-by? We can shake, shake, shake.

1 + 2 + 3 + 4 + 1 + 2 + 3 + 4 +

N.C. |G |

Yeah, oh. 'Cause the

Chorus

① + ② + ③ + ④ + ① + ② + ③ + ④ + ① + ② + ③ + ④ + ① + ② + ③ + ④ +

Em | |G |

play-ers gon-na play, play, play, play, play, and the hat-ers gon-na hate, hate, hate, hate, hate, ba-by.

① + ② + ③ + ④ + ① + ② + ③ + ④ + ① + ② + ③ + ④ + ① + ② + ③ + ④ +

D | | |

I'm just gon-na shake, shake, shake, shake, shake; I shake it off, I shake it off. Heart-

① + ② + ③ + ④ + ① + ② + ③ + ④ + ① + ② + ③ + ④ + ① + ② + ③ + ④ +

Em | |G |

break-ers gon-na break, break, break, break, break and the fak-ers gon-na fake, fake, fake, fake, fake, ba-by.

① + ② + ③ + ④ + ① + ② + ③ + ④ + ① + ② + ③ + ④ + ① + ② + ③ + ④ +

D | | |

I'm just gon-na shake, shake, shake, shake, shake; I shake it off, I shake it off. I

Outro

① + ② + ③ + ④ + ① + ② + ③ + ④ + ① + ② + ③ + ④ + ① + ② + ③ + ④ +

|:Em | |G |

shake it off, I shake it off. I, I, I shake, it off, I shake it off. I, I, I

① + ② + ③ + ④ + ① + ② + ③ + ④ + ① + ② + ③ + ④ +

D | | |

shake it off, I shake it off. I, I, I shake it off, I shake it

1.

① + ② + ③ + ④ +

2.

① + 2 + 3 + 4 + 1 + 2 + 3 + 4 +

:| ||

off. I off. Ah.

Viva La Vida

Performed by Coldplay
Arranged by NYC Guitar School

Words and Music by Guy Berryman,
Jon Buckland, Will Champion and Chris Martin

C   D   G   Em

Intro

① ② ③ ④ ① ② ③ ④ ① ② ③ ④ ① ② ③ ④

C |**D** |**G** |**Em** |

① ② ③ ④ ① ② ③ ④ ① ② ③ ④ ① ② ③ ④

C |**D** |**G** |**Em** |**C** |

I used to rule the world.

Verse 1

① ② ③ ④ ① ② ③ ④ ① ② ③ ④ ① ② ③ ④

D |**G** |**Em** |**C** |

Seas would rise when I gave the word. Now in the morn-ing I sleep a-lone,

① ② ③ ④ ① ② ③ ④ ① ② ③ ④

D |**G** |**Em** |

sweep the streets I used to own.

Interlude

① ② ③ ④ ① ② ③ ④ ① ② ③ ④ ① ② ③ ④

|:**C** |**D** |**G** |**Em**   :|

(2nd time:) I used to

Verse 2 & 3

① ② ③ ④ ① ② ③ ④ ① ② ③ ④ ① ② ③ ④

|:**C** |**D** |**G** |**Em** |

roll the dice, feel the fear in my en-e-mies eyes. Lis-ten as the
held the key, next the walls were closed on me. And I dis-cov-ered that my

① ② ③ ④ ① ② ③ ④ ① ② ③ ④ ① ② ③ ④

C |**D** |**G** |**Em**   :|

crowd would sing, "Now the old king is dead, long live the king" One min-ute I
cas - tles stand up-on pil-lars of salt and pil-lars of sand. I

Chorus

|: **C** | **D** | **G** | **Em** |

hear Je - ru - sa - lem bells a ring - ring, Ro - man Cav - al - ry choirs are sing - ing.
For some rea - son I can't ex - plain. Once you'd gone there was nev - er, nev - er an

C | **D** | **G** | **Em** :|

Be my mir - ror, my sword and shield, my mis - sion - ar - ies in a for - eign field.
hon - est word. And that was when I ruled the world.

Interlude

|: **C** | **D** | **G** | **Em** :|

(2nd time:) It was a wick - ed and wild

Verse 4 & 5

|: **C** | **D** | **G** | **Em** |

wind, blew down the doors to let me in. Shat - tered win - dows and the
ar - ies wait for my head on a sil - ver plate. Just a pup - pet on a

C | **D** | **G** | **Em** :|

sound of drums. Peo - ple could - n't be - lieve what I'd be - come. Rev - o - lu - tion -
lone - ly string. Ah, who would ev - er wan - na be king? I

Chorus

|: **C** | **D** | **G** | **Em** |

hear Je - ru - sa - lem bells a ring - ring, Ro - man Cav - al - ry choirs are sing - ing.
For some rea - son I can't ex - plain. I know Saint Pe - ter won't call my name, nev - er an

C | **D** | **G** | **Em** :|

Be my mir - ror, my sword and shield, my mis - sion - ar - ies in a for - eign field.
hon - est word. But that was when I ruled the world.

Bridge

‖: C | Em :‖ C | Em | D | |

Oh,

‖: C | D | G | Em :‖

oh,
oh,

oh.
oh.

Chorus

C | D | G | Em |

Hear Je - ru - sa - lem bells a ring - ring, Ro - man Cav - al - ry choirs are sing - ing.

C | D | G | Em |

Be my mir - ror, my sword and shield, my mis - sion - ar - ies in a for - eign field.

C | D | G | Em |

For some rea - son I can't ex - plain. I know Saint Pe - ter won't call my name, nev - er an

C | D | G | Em |

hon - est word. But that was when I ruled the world.

Outro

‖: C | D | G | Em :‖ G |

We're Going to Be Friends

Performed by The White Stripes
Arranged by NYC Guitar School

Words and Music by
Jack White

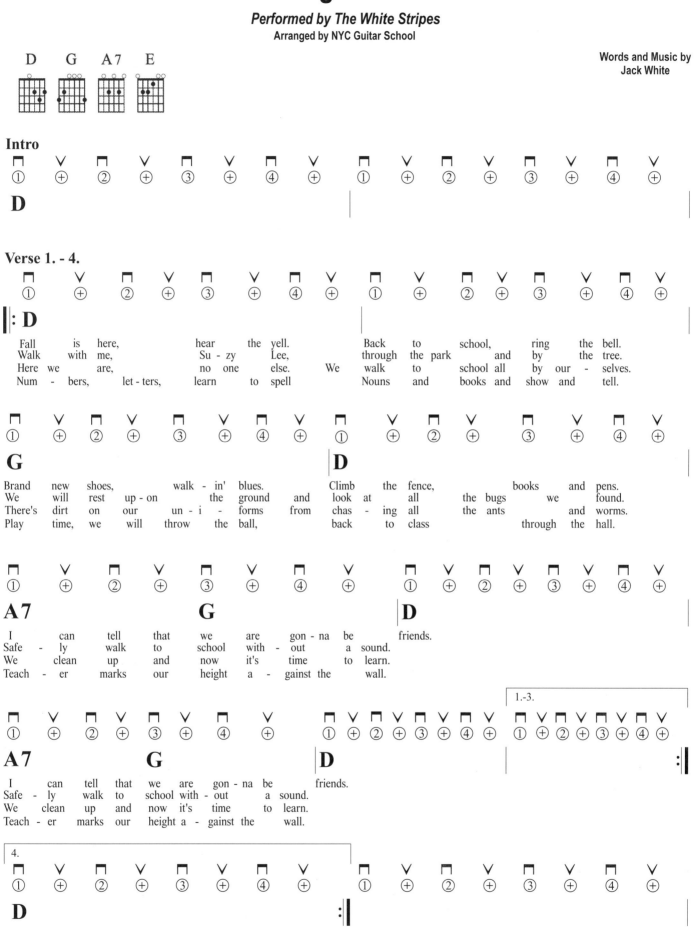

Bridge

⊓ V ⊓ V ⊓ V ⊓ V ⊓ V ⊓ V ⊓ V ⊓ V
① + ② + ③ + ④ + ① + ② + ③ + ④ +

G | **D** |

We don't no - tice an y time. pass.

⊓ V ⊓ V ⊓ V ⊓ V ⊓ V ⊓ V ⊓ V ⊓ V
① + ② + ③ + ④ + ① + ② + ③ + ④ +

G | **D** |

We don't no - tice an - y - thing.

⊓ V ⊓ V ⊓ V ⊓ V ⊓ V ⊓ V ⊓ V ⊓ V
① + ② + ③ + ④ + ① + ② + ③ + ④ +

E | |

We sit side by side in ev - 'ry class.

⊓ V ⊓ V ⊓ V ⊓ V ⊓ V ⊓ V ⊓ V ⊓ V
① + ② + ③ + ④ + ① + ② + ③ + ④ +

G |**A7** |

Teach - er thinks that I sound fun - ny but she likes the way you sing. To -

Verse 5

⊓ V ⊓ V ⊓ V ⊓ V ⊓ V ⊓ V ⊓ V ⊓ V
① + ② + ③ + ④ + ① + ② + ③ + ④ +

D | |

night I'll dream while I'm in bed with sil - ly thoughts go through my head

⊓ V ⊓ V ⊓ V ⊓ V ⊓ V ⊓ V ⊓ V ⊓ V
① + ② + ③ + ④ + ① + ② + ③ + ④ +

G |**D** |

'bout the bugs and al - pha - bet, and when I wake to - mor - row, I'll bet that

⊓ V ⊓ V ⊓ V ⊓ V ⊓ V ⊓ V ⊓ V ⊓ V
① + ② + ③ + ④ + ① + ② + ③ + ④ +

A7 **G** **D** |

you and I will walk to - geth - er a - gain.

⊓ V ⊓ V ⊓ V ⊓ V ⊓ V ⊓ V ⊓ V ⊓ V
① + ② + ③ + ④ + ① + ② + ③ + ④ +

A7 **G** |**D** |

I can tell that we are gon - na be friends. Yes,

⊓ V ⊓ V ⊓ V ⊓ V ⊓
① + ② + ③ + ④ + ① + 2 + 3 + 4 +

A7 **G** |**D** ‖

I can tell that we are gon - na be friends.

31

Zombie

Performed by The Cranberries
Arranged by NYC Guitar School

Lyrics and Music by
Dolores O'Riordan

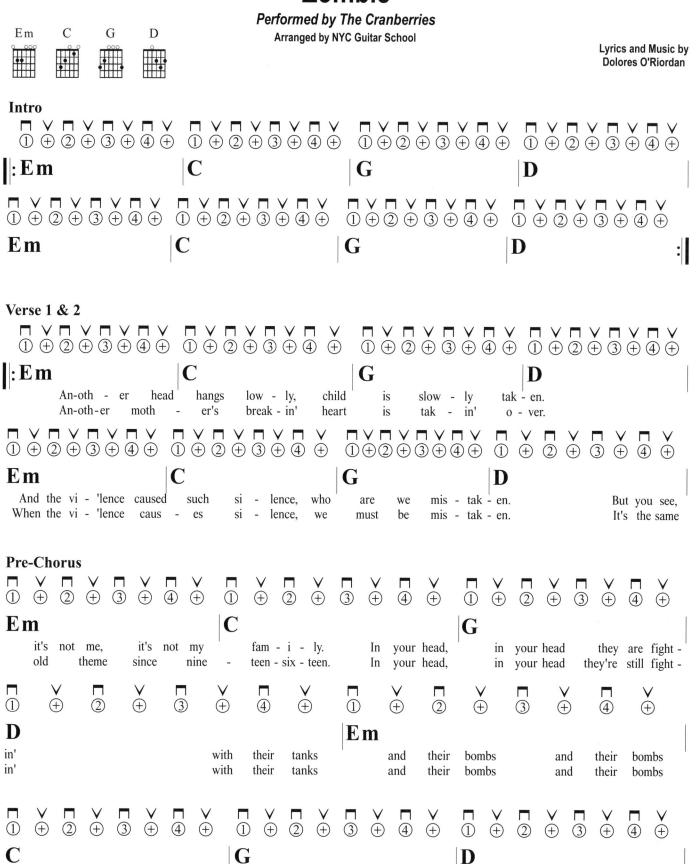

Chorus

□ V □ V □ V □ V | □ V □ V □ V □ V | □ V □ V □ V □ V | □ V □ V □ V □ V
① + ② + ③ + ④ + | ① + ② + ③ + ④ + | ① + ② + ③ + ④ + | ① + ② + ③ + ④ +

Em | **C** | **G** | **D** |

head,   in your head,   zom - bie,   zom - bie,   zom - bie,   eh,   eh.   What's in your
head,   in your head,   zom - bie,   zom - bie,   zom - bie,   hey,   hey.   What's in your

□ V □ V □ V □ V | □ V □ V □ V □ V | □ V □ V □ V □ V | □ V □ V □ V □ V
① + ② + ③ + ④ + | ① + ② + ③ + ④ + | ① + ② + ③ + ④ + | ① + ② + ③ + ④ +

Em | **C** | **G** | **D** |

head,   in your head,   zom - bie,   zom - bie,   zom - bie,   eh,   eh,   eh?   Oh,
head,   in your head,   zom - bie,   zom - bie,   zom - bie,   hey,   hey,   hey?   Oh,

□ V □ V □ V □ V | □ V □ V □ V □ V | □ V □ V □ V □ V | □ V □ V □ V □ V
① + ② + ③ + ④ + | ① + ② + ③ + ④ + | ① + ② + ③ + ④ + | ① + ② + ③ + ④ +

Em | **C** | **G** | **D** |

do,   do,   do,   do,   do,   do,   do,   do,   do,   do,   do,   do,   do,   do,   do,   do.
oh,   oh,   oh,   oh,   oh,   oh,   hey,   oh,   ya, ya.

□ V □ V □ V □ V | □ V □ V □ V □ V | □ V □ V □ V □ V | □ V □ V □ V □ V
① + ② + ③ + ④ + | ① + ② + ③ + ④ + | ① + ② + ③ + ④ + | ① + ② + ③ + ④ +

Em | **C** | **G** | **D** :|

Guitar Solo

□ V □ V □ V □ V | □ V □ V □ V □ V | □ V □ V □ V □ V | □ V □ V □ V □ V
① + ② + ③ + ④ + | ① + ② + ③ + ④ + | ① + ② + ③ + ④ + | ① + ② + ③ + ④ +

||: **Em** | **C** | **Em** | **C** :|

□ V □ V □ V □ V | □ V □ V □ V □ V | □ V □ V □ V □ V | □ V □ V □ V □ V
① + ② + ③ + ④ + | ① + ② + ③ + ④ + | ① + ② + ③ + ④ + | ① + ② + ③ + ④ +

||: **Em** | **C** | **G** | **D** :|

□ V □ V □ V □ V | □ V □ V □ V □ V | □ V □ V □ V □ V | □ V □ V □ V □ V
① + ② + ③ + ④ + | ① + ② + ③ + ④ + | ① + ② + ③ + ④ + | ① + ② + ③ + ④ +

Em | **C** | **G** | **D** :|

Outro

□ V □ V □ V □ V | □ V □ V □ V □ V | □ V □ V □ V □ V | □ V □ V □ V □ V
① + ② + ③ + ④ + | ① + ② + ③ + ④ + | ① + ② + ③ + ④ + | ① + ② + ③ + ④ +

Em | **C** | **Em** | **C** |

□ V □ V □ V □ V | □ V □ V □ V □ V | □ V □ V □ V □ V
① + ② + ③ + ④ + | ① + ② + ③ + ④ + | ① + 2 + 3 + 4 +

Em | **C** | **Em** |

Jolene

Performed by Dolly Parton
Arranged by NYC Guitar School

Words and Music by
Dolly Parton

Am   C   G

Intro

Am

Jo -

% Chorus

Am | C | G | Am | G |

lene,   Jo - lene,   Jo - lene,   Jo - lene,   I'm beg-ging of you, please don't take

Am | | | | C | G |

my man.   Jo - lene,   Jo - lene,   Jo - lene,   Jo -

Am | G | | Am | | |

lene,   please don't take him   just be-cause you   can.   Your

Verse 1 & 3

Am | C | G | Am | G |

beau - ty is be - yond com-pare, with   flam - ing locks of   au - burn hair, with   i - v'ry skin   and eyes of em' - rald
You could have your choice of men, but   I could nev - er   love a - gain.   He's the on - ly one for me, Jo -

Am | |

green.
lene.   Your smile is like a
                                             I had to have this

C | G | Am | G |

breath of spring, your   voice is soft like   sum - mer rain, and   I can - not com - pete with you,
talk with you; my   hap - pi - ness de - pends on   you and   what - ev - er you   de - cide to do,

To Coda ⊕

Am | | | |

        Jo - lene.   He
        Jo - lene.   Jo -

Verse 2

Am |C |G |Am |G |

talks a - bout you in his sleep and there's noth - ing I can do to keep from cry - in' when he

G |Am |

calls your name, Jo - lene.   And I can eas - 'ly

C |G |Am |G |

un - der - stand how you could eas - 'ly take my man, but you don't know what he means to me, Jo -

D.S. al Coda

Am |

lene.   Jo -

Chorus

Am |C |G |Am |

lene,   Jo - lene,   Jo - lene,   Jo - lene,   I'm

G |Am |

beg - ging of you, please don't take my man.

              |C |G |Am |

Jo - lene,   Jo - lene,   Jo - lene,   Jo - lene,

         |G |

please don't take him e - ven - though you

Am |

can.   Jo -

Outro

Am |

lene.   (Jo - lene.)

Knockin' on Heaven's Door

Performed by Bob Dylan
Arranged by NYC Guitar School

Words and Music by
Bob Dylan

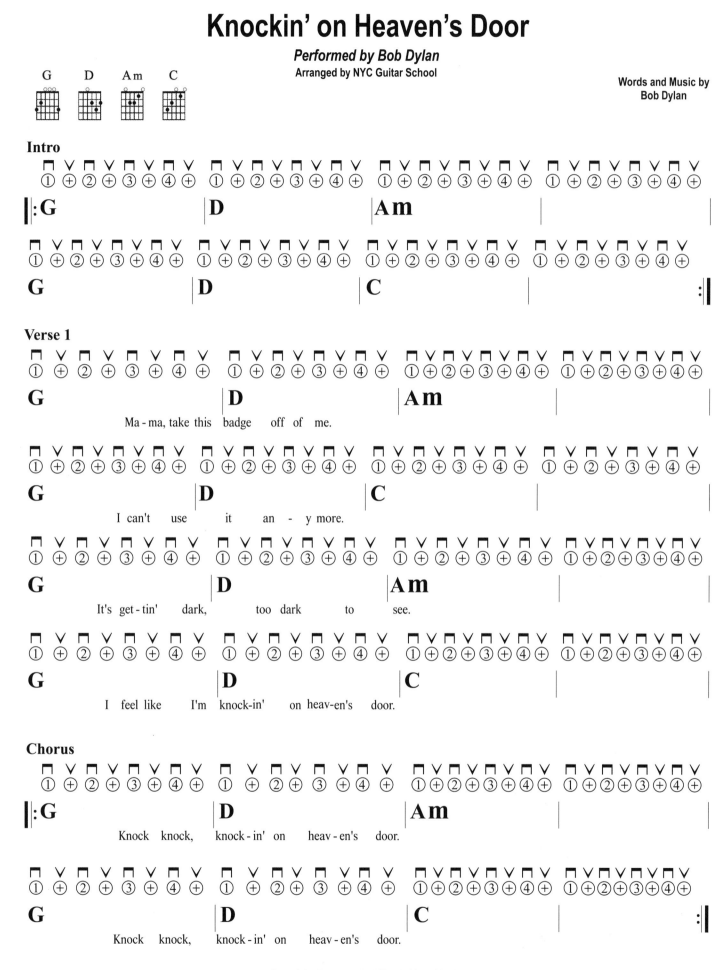

Verse 2

G | D | Am | |

Ma - ma, put my guns in the ground.

G | D | C | |

I can't shoot them an - y more.

G | D | Am | |

That long black cloud is com-in' down.

G | D | C | |

I feel like I'm knock-in' on heav-en's door.

Chorus

‖: G | D | Am | |

Knock knock, knock - in' on heav - en's door.

G | D | C | | :‖

Knock knock, knock - in' on heav - en's door.

Outro

G | D | Am | |

G | D | Am | ‖

The Only Exception

Performed by Paramore
Arranged by NYC Guitar School

Words and Music by Hayley Williams
and Josh Farro

D Am G Em A C

Intro

① ② ① ② ① ② ① ②

|: D | |Am |G :|

Verse 1

① ② ① ② ① ② ① ②

D | |Am |G |

When I was young-er, I saw my dad-dy cry and curse at the wind. He

① ② ① ② ① ② ① ②

D | |Am |G |

broke his own heart and I watched as he tried to re - as-sem - ble it. And

① ② ① ② ① ② ① ②

D | |Am |G |

my ma - ma swore that she would nev-er let her - self forget. And

① ② ① ② ① ② ① ②

D | |Am |G |

that was the day that I prom-ised I'd nev-er sing of love if it does not ex - ist. But dar-ling,

𝄋 Chorus

① ② ① ② ① ② ① ②

D | |Am |G |

you are the on - ly ex - cep-tion. Oh, you are the on - ly ex - cep-tion. Oh,

To Coda ⊕

① ② ① ② ① ② ① ②

D | |Am |G |

you are the on - ly ex - cep-tion. Oh, you are the on - ly ex - cep-tion.

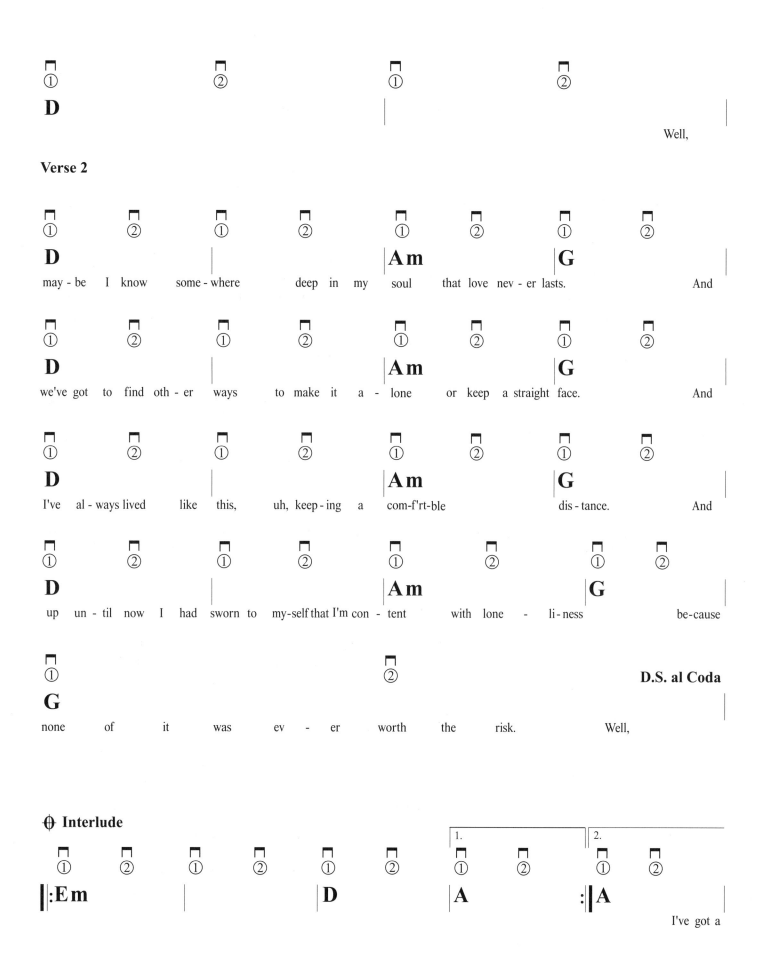

Verse 2

D | | Am | G
may - be I know some - where deep in my soul that love nev - er lasts. And

D | | Am | G
we've got to find oth - er ways to make it a - lone or keep a straight face. And

D | | Am | G
I've al - ways lived like this, uh, keep - ing a com-f'rt-ble dis - tance. And

D | | Am | G
up un - til now I had sworn to my-self that I'm con - tent with lone - li - ness be-cause

D.S. al Coda

G |
none of it was ev - er worth the risk. Well,

Interlude

1.   2.
‖:Em | | D |A :‖A |
I've got a

Bridge

Em | D | A |

tight grip on re-al - i - ty, but I can't let go of what's in front of me here. I know you're

Em | D |

leav - ing in the morn-ing when you wake up. Leave me with some kind of proof it's not a

A | G |

dream, oh.

Chorus

‖: D | Am | G |

You are the on - ly ex - cep-tion. Oh, you are the on - ly ex - cep-tion. Oh,

D | Am | G :‖

you are the on - ly ex - cep-tion. Oh, you are the on - ly ex - cep-tion.

Outro

C | G |

I'm on my way to be - liev - ing.

D | C | G |

Oh, and I'm on my way to be - liev - ing.

D |

40

We Are Young

Performed by fun.
Arranged by NYC Guitar School

**Words and Music by
Jeff Bhasker, Andrew Dost,
Jack Antonoff and Nate Ruess**

G   Em   Am   C   D

Verse 1

① 2 3 4 1 2 3 4

G

Give me a sec-ond I, I need to get my sto-ry straight. My

① 2 3 4 1 2 3 4

Em

friends are in the bath-room get-ting high-er than the Em-pire State. My

① 2 3 4 1 2 3 4

Am

lov-er, she's wait-ing for me just a-cross the bar. My seat's been

① 2 3 4 ① 2 3 4

C   **D**

tak-en by some sun-glass-es ask-in' 'bout a scar. And

① ② ③ ④ ① ② ③ ④

G

I know I gave it to you months a-go;

① ② ③ ④ ① ② ③ ④

Em

I know you're try-ing to for-get. But be-

① ② ③ ④ ① ② ③ ④

Am

tween the drinks and sub-tle things, the holes in my a-pol-o-gies, you know,we

① ② ③ ④ ① ② ③ ④

C   **D**

I'm try-ing hard to take it back. So, if by the

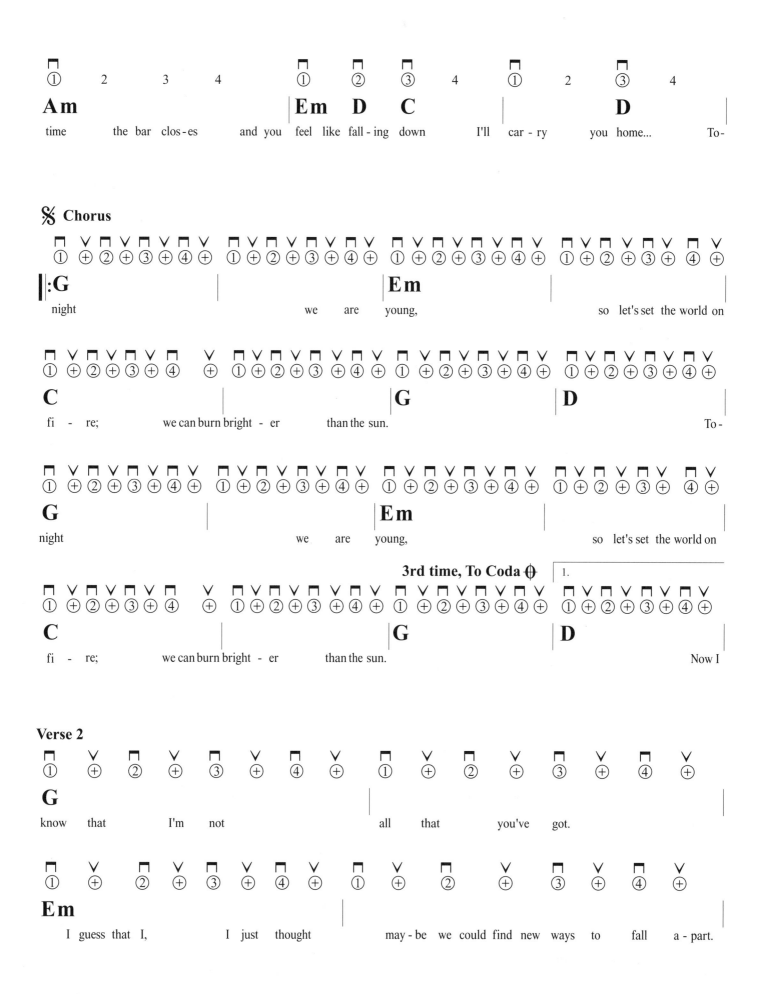

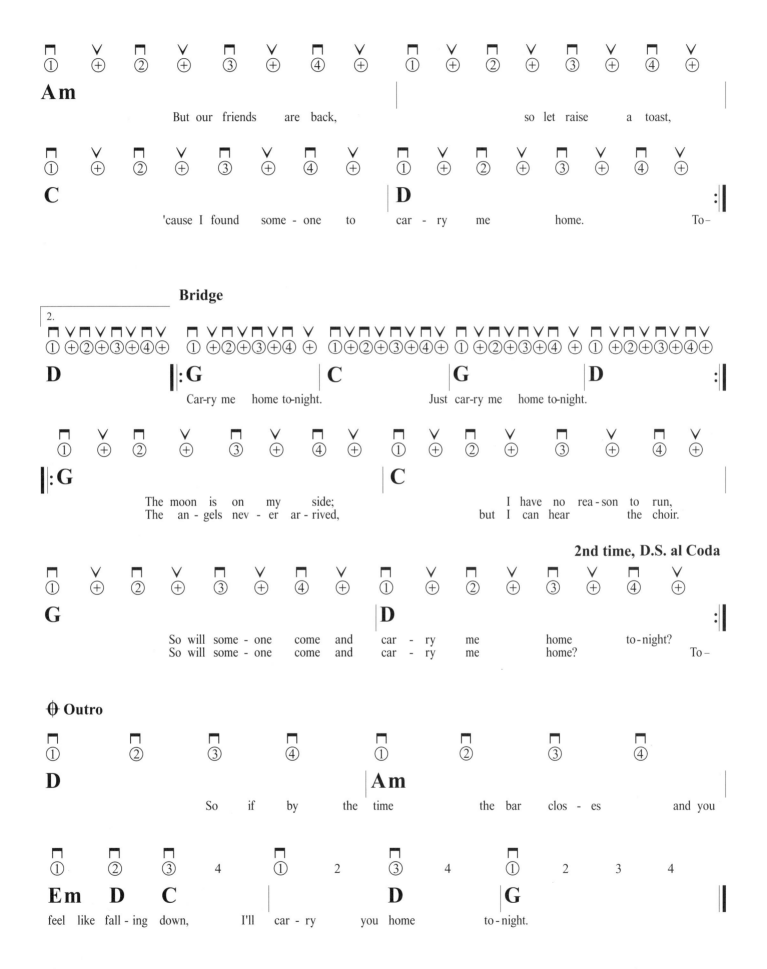

Capo IV

I'm Yours

Performed by Jason Mraz

Arranged by NYC Guitar School

Words and Music by
Jason Mraz

G   Em   C   D

Intro

3 + 4 + ① + ② + ③ + ④ + ① + ② + ③ + ④ + ① + ② + ③ + ④ + ① + ② + ③ + ④ +

|G | |D |

① + ② + ③ + ④ + ① + ② + ③ + ④ + ① + ② + ③ + ④ + ① + ② + ③ + ④ +

Em | |C |

Well,

𝄋 Verse 1 & 3

① + ② + ③ + ④ + ① + ② + ③ + ④ + ① + ② + ③ + ④ + ① + ② + ③ + ④ +

G | |D |

you done done me in; you bet I felt it. I tried to be chill, but you're so hot that I melt - ed. I
way too long check-ing my tongue in the mir-ror and bend-ing o - ver back-wards just to try to see it clear-er. But

① + ② + ③ + ④ + ① + ② + ③ + ④ + ① + ② + ③ + ④ + ① + ② + ③ + ④ +

Em | |C |

fell right through the cracks. Now I'm try - ing to get back. Be-fore the
my breath fogged up the glass, and so I drew a new face and I laughed. I

① + ② + ③ + ④ + ① + ② + ③ + ④ + ① + ② + ③ + ④ + ① + ② + ③ + ④ +

G | |D |

cool done run out, I'll be giv-ing it my best-est, and noth-ing's gon-na stop me but di - vine in - ter - ven - tion. I
guess what I'll be say-ing is there ain't no bet - ter rea-son to rid your-self of van - i - ties and just go with the sea-sons. It's

① + ② + ③ + ④ + ① + ② + ③ + ④ + ① + ② + ③ + ④ + ① + ② + ③ + ④ +

Em | |C |

reck - on it's a - gain my turn to win some or learn some. } But
what we aim to do. Our name is our vir - tue.

Chorus

G | | D | |

I won't hes - i - tate no more, no

To Coda ⊕

Em | | C | |

more. It can - not wait. I'm yours.

G | | D | |

Em | | C | |

Verse 2

G | | D | |

Well, o - pen up your mind and see like me. O - pen up your plans and, damn, you're free.

Em | | C | |

I look in - to your heart and you'll find love, love, love love.

G | | D | |

Lis - ten to the mu - sic of the mo - ment; peo - ple dance and sing. We're just one big fam - i - ly,

Em | | C | |

and it's our god - for - sak - en right to be loved, loved,

□ □ ∨ □ □ ∨ □ □ ∨ □ □ ∨ □ □ ∨ □ □ ∨
① + ② + ③ + ④ ⊕ ① + ② + ③ + ④ ⊕ ① + ② + ③ + ④ ⊕

|**A7** |

loved,   loved.   loved,   So,

Chorus

□ □ ∨ □ □ ∨ □ □ ∨ □ □ ∨ □ □ ∨ □ □ ∨ □ ∨ □ ∨
① + ② + ③ + ④ ⊕ ① + ② + ③ + ④ ⊕ ① + ② + ③ + ④ ⊕ ① + ② + ③ + ④ ⊕

G | |**D** |

I   won't   hes - i - tate   no   more,   no

□ □ ∨ □ □ ∨ □ □ ∨ □ □ ∨ □ □ ∨ □ □ ∨ □ □ ∨ □ ∨
① + ② + ③ + ④ ⊕ ① + ② + ③ + ④ ⊕ ① + ② + ③ + ④ ⊕ ① + ② + ③ + ④ ⊕

Em | |**C** |

more.   It   can - not   wait.   I'm   sure   there's no

□ □ ∨ □ □ ∨ □ □ ∨ □ □ ∨ □ □ ∨ □ □ ∨ □ □ ∨ □ ∨
① + ② + ③ + ④ ⊕ ① + ② + ③ + ④ ⊕ ① + ② + ③ + ④ ⊕ ① + ② + ③ + ④ ⊕

G | |**D** |

need   to   com - pli - cate.   Our   time   is

□ □ ∨ □ □ ∨ □ □ ∨ □ □ ∨ □ □ ∨ □ □ ∨ □ □ ∨ □ ∨
① + ② + ③ + ④ ⊕ ① + ② + ③ + ④ ⊕ ① + ② + ③ + ④ ⊕ ① + ② + ③ + ④ ⊕

Em | |**C** |

short.   This   is   our   fate.   I'm   yours.

Bridge

□ □ ∨ □ □ ∨ □ □ ∨ □ □ ∨ □ □ ∨ □ □ ∨ □ □ ∨ □ ∨
① + ② + ③ + ④ ⊕ ① + ② + ③ + ④ ⊕ ① + ② + ③ + ④ ⊕ ① + ② + ③ + ④ ⊕

G |**D** |**Em** |**D** |

Scat...   Do you want to come on,   schooch on o - ver

□ □ ∨ □ □ ∨ □ □ ∨ □ □ ∨ □ □ ∨ □ □ ∨ □ □ ∨ □ ∨
① + ② + ③ + ④ ⊕ ① + ② + ③ + ④ ⊕ ① + ② + ③ + ④ ⊕ ① + ② + ③ + ④ ⊕

C | |**A7** |

clo - ser,   dear,   and I will nib - ble your ear.

G | D | Em | D |

D.S. al Coda

C | A7 |

I've been spend-ing

Verse 4

C | G |

yours.　　Well, o - pen up your mind　and see　like　me.

D | Em |

O - pen up your plans - and, damn, you're free.　Look in - to your heart　and you'll find　that

C | G |

the　sky　is　yours.　So　please　don't,　please don't,　please　don't.　There's no

D | Em |

need　to com - pli - cate　'cause our　time　is　short.　This is, this is, this is　our

C | A7 |

fate.　I'm　yours.

Outro

|: G | D |

Em | C :|

47

Ticket to Ride

Performed by The Beatles
Arranged by NYC Guitar School

Words and Music by
John Lennon and Paul McCartney

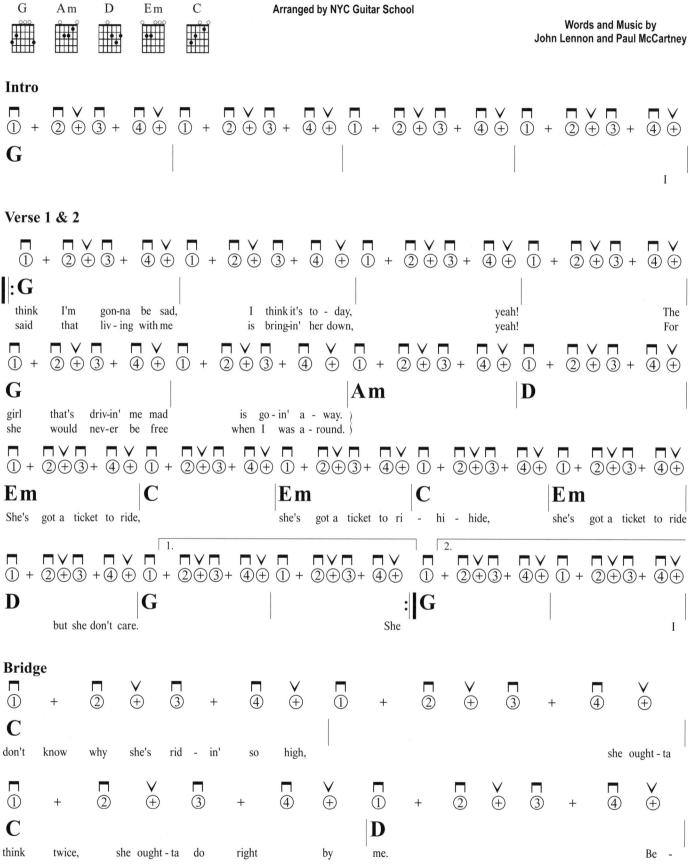

C

fore she gets to say - in' good - bye, she ought - ta

C |D

think twice, she ought-ta do right   by   me.   I

Verse 3

G

think   I'm   gon-na be sad,   I   think it's to - day,   yeah!   The

G |Am |D

girl   that's driv-in' me mad   is go-in' a - way,   yeah!   Ah!

Em |C |Em |C

She's   got a tick-et to ride,   she's   got a tick-et to ri - hi - hide,

Em |D |G |

she's   got a tick-et to ride   but she don't care.   I

Bridge

C

don't know   why she's rid - in' so   high,   she ought - ta

C |D

think   twice,   she ought - ta do   right   by   me.   Be -

① + ② ⊕ ③ + ④ ⊕ ① + ② ⊕ ③ + ④ ⊕

C

fore she gets to say - in' good - bye, she ought - ta

① + ② ⊕ ③ + ④ ⊕ ① + ② ⊕ ③ + ④ ⊕ ① + ② ⊕ ③ + ④ ⊕

C | **D**

think twice, she ought-ta do right by me. She

Verse 3

① + ② + ③ + ④ ⊕ ① + ② + ③ + ④ ⊕ ① + ② + ③ + ④ ⊕ ① + ② + ③ + ④ ⊕

G

said that liv - ing with me is bring-in' her down, yeah! For

① + ② + ③ + ④ ⊕ ① + ② + ③ + ④ ⊕ ① + ② + ③ + ④ ⊕ ① + ② + ③ + ④ ⊕

G | **Am** | **D**

she would nev-er be free when I was a - round. Ah!

① + ② + ③ + ④ ⊕ ① + ② + ③ + ④ ⊕ ① + ② + ③ + ④ ⊕ ① + ② + ③ + ④ ⊕

Em | **C** | **Em** | **C**

She's got a tick-et to ride, she's got a tick-et to ri - hi - hide,

① + ② ⊕ ③ + ④ ⊕ ① + ② ⊕ ③ + ④ ⊕

Em | **D**

she's got a tick - et to ride but she don't care.

Outro

① + ② + ③ + ④ ⊕ ① + ② + ③ + ④ ⊕ ① + ② + ③ + ④ ⊕ ① + ② + ③ + ④ ⊕

G

My ba - by don't care. My ba - by don't

① + ② ⊕ ③ + ④ ⊕ ① + ② ⊕ ③ + 4 +

G

care.

Capo II

Wonderwall

Performed by Oasis
Arranged by NYC Guitar School

Words and Music by
Noel Gallagher

Em G D A7 C

Intro

|: Em   G | D   A7 | Em   G | D   A7   :|

Verse 1 & 2

|: Em   G | D   A7 |

To - day   is gon - na be the day   that they're gon - na throw it   back to you.
Back - beat   the word was on the street   that the   fire   in your heart is out.

Em   G | D   A7 |

By   now   you should - 've some how   re - al - ized   what you got - ta do.   )
I'm   sure   you've heard it all be - fore,   but you   nev - er   real - ly had   a doubt.)

Em   G | D   A7 |

I don't be - lieve   that an - y - bod - y   feels   the way   I   do   a - bout   you now.

1.

C   D | A7   :|

the roads we have to walk are wind - ing,

2.

Em   G | D   A7 |

And all

Chorus

|: C   D | Em | C   D |

the roads we have   to walk   are wind - ing,   and all   the lights that lead us there are blind
the roads that lead   you there were wind - ing,   and all   the lights that light the way are blind -

Em | C | D | G | D | Em | G |

– ing.   There are man - y   things that I   would   like   to say   to you,   but I   don't know
– ing.   There are man - y   things that I   would   like   to say   to you,   but I   don't know

A7 | | C | Em |

how.
how.   Be - cause)   may - be
            I   said)

G | Em | C | Em | G | Em |

you're gon - na be the one that saves me,   and af - ter   all,

To Coda ⊕

C | Em | G | Em | C | Em |

you're my won - der - wall.

G | Em |

Verse 3

Em | G | D | A7 |

To - day   was gon - na be the day   but they'll nev - ver throw it back to you.

Em | G | D | A7 |

By   now   you should - 've some how re - al - ized   what you're not to do.

Em | G | D | A7 |

I don't be - lieve   that an - y - bod - y   feels   the way   I   do   a - bout you now.

Em | G | D | A7 | :||

And all

Outro

G   Em |C   Em |

I said   may - be

G   Em |C   Em |

you're gon - na be the one   that   saves   me,

G   Em |C   Em |G   Em |

and af - ter   all,   you're my won - der - wall.

C   Em |G   Em |

I said

C   Em |G   Em |

may - be   you're gon - na be the one   that

C   Em |G   Em |

saves   me,   you're gon - na be the one   that

C   Em |G   Em |

saves   me,   you're gon - na be the one   that

C   Em |G   Em |G   Em |

saves me.

All of Me

Performed by John Legend
Arranged by NYC Guitar School

Words and Music by
John Stephens and Toby Gad

Em C G D Am

Intro

| Em | C | G | D |

Verse

‖: Em | C

What would I   do with - out   your   smart
How man - y   times do I   have to tell

G | D

mouth   draw - in' me   in and you   kick - ing me   out?
you,   e - ven when you're   cry - ing, you're   beau - ti - ful   too?

Em | C

You've got my   head   spin - nin'
The world is   beat   -   ing you

G | D

no   kid - din'.   I   can't   pin you   down.
down.   I'm   a - round   through   ev - er - y   mood.

Em | C

What's go - in'   on   in   that   beau - ti - ful   mind?
You're   my   down - fall,   you're   my   muse,

G | D

I'm   on   your   mag - i - cal   mys - ter - y   ride.
my   worst   dis - trac - tion,   my   rhy - thm and   blues.

① + ② ⊕ ③ + ④ ⊕ ① + ② ⊕ ③ + ④ ⊕

Em | **C**

And I'm so diz - zy; don't
I can't stop sing - in', it's

① + ② ⊕ ③ + ④ ⊕ ① + ② ⊕ ③ + ④ ⊕

G | **D**

know what hit me. But I'll be al -
ring - in' in my head for you.

Pre-Chorus

① + ② + ③ + ④ ⊕ ① + ② ⊕ ③ + ④ ⊕ ① + ② ⊕ ③ + ④ ⊕ ① + ② ⊕ ③ + ④ ⊕

Am | | **G** | **D**

right.) My head's un - der wa - ter, but I'm breath - ing fine.

① + ② ⊕ ③ + ④ ⊕ ① + ② ⊕ ③ + ④ ⊕ ① + ② ⊕ ③ + ④ ⊕ ① + ② ⊕ ③ + ④ ⊕

Am | | **G** | **D**

You're cra - zy and I'm out of my mind. 'Cause

𝄋 **Chorus**

① + ② ⊕ ③ + ④ ⊕ ① + ② ⊕ ③ + ④ ⊕ ① + ② ⊕ ③ + ④ ⊕ ① + ② ⊕ ③ + ④ ⊕

G | **Em** |

all of me loves all of you. Love your

① + ② ⊕ ③ + ④ ⊕ ① + ② ⊕ ③ + ④ ⊕ ① + ② ⊕ ③ + ④ ⊕ ① + ② ⊕ ③ + ④ ⊕

C | | **D**

curves and all your edg - es, all your per - fect im - per-fec - tions. Give your

① + ② ⊕ ③ + ④ ⊕ ① + ② ⊕ ③ + ④ ⊕ ① + ② ⊕ ③ + ④ ⊕ ① + ② ⊕ ③ + ④ ⊕

G | **Em** |

all to me, I'll give my all to you. You're my

① + ② ⊕ ③ + ④ ⊕ ① + ② ⊕ ③ + ④ ⊕ ① + ② ⊕ ③ + ④ ⊕ ① + ② ⊕ ③ + ④ ⊕

C | | **D**

end and my be - gin - ning. E - ven when I lose, I'm win - ning. 'Cause I give you all

Em | C | G | D |

of me, and you give me all

To Coda ⊕

1.

Em | C | G | D | :||

of you. Oh.

Bridge

2.

G | D | Am |

Oh. Give me all of you. Cards on the ta-

G | D | Am |

- ble, we're both show - ing hearts. Risk - ing it all,

D.S. al Coda

G | D |

though it's hard. 'Cause

⊕ Outro

G | D | Em | C |

I give you all of me,

G | D | Em | C |

and you give me all of you.

G | D |

Oh.

This page has been intentionally left blank to facilitate page turns.

Brown Eyed Girl

Performed by Van Morrison
Arranged by NYC Guitar School

Words and Music by
Van Morrison

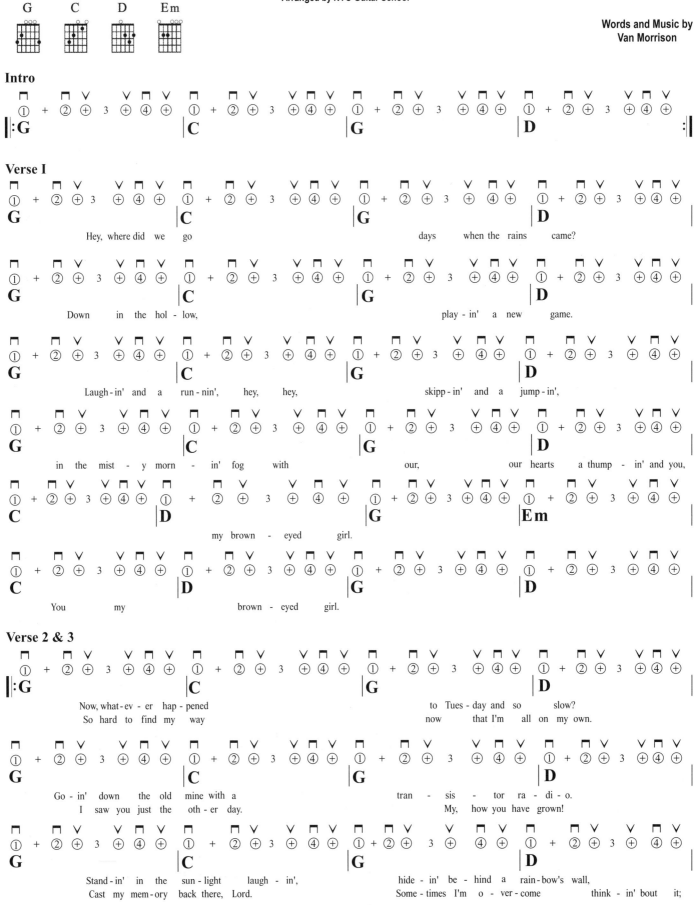

G | C | G | D

slip - pin' and a slid in' / all a - long the wa - ter - fall with you,
mak - in' love in the green grass / be - hind the sta - di - um - with you,

C | D | G | Em

my brown - eyed girl.)
my brown - eyed girl.)

C | D

You my brown - eyed girl.

G | D

Do you re - mem - ber when we used to sing?

Chorus

G | C | G | D

Sha, la, la, la, la, la, la, la, la, la, la, te da. Just like that.

G | C | G | D

Sha, la, la, la, la, la, la, la, la, la, la, te da. La, te, da.

Interlude

1.

G

G | C | G | D

Outro

2.

G | C | G | D

Sha, la, la, la, la, la, la, la, la, la, la, te da.

G | C | G | D

Sha, la, la, la, la, la, la, la, la, la, la, te, da. La, te, da.

Fight Song

Performed by Rachel Platten
Arranged by NYC Guitar School

Words and Music by
Rachel Platten and Dave Bassett

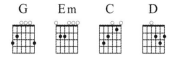

Verse 1

G

Like a small boat   on the o - cean

send - ing big waves   in - to mo - tion.   Like how a sin - gle word

Em   C   G

can make a heart o - pen,   I might on-ly have one match   that I can make an ex - plo - sion.   And all those

Pre-Chorus

G   C   D   Em

things I did - n't say were wreck - ing balls   in - side my brain,   and I will scream

G   C   D

'em a - loud to - night.   Can you hear my voice this time? This is my

Chorus

G   D   Em

fight song,   take back my life song,   prove I'm al - right song.

C   G   D

My pow - er's turned on.   Start-ing right now I'll be strong.   I'll play my

To Coda ⊕

Em   C   Em   D

fight song.   And I don't real - ly care if no - bod - y else be - lieves   'cause

C   G

I've still got a lot of fight left in me.

Verse 2

Em | C | G |

Los - in' friends and I'm chas - in' sleep. Ev - 'ry - bod - y's wor - ried 'bout me, in too deep, say I'm

D | Em | C |

in too deep, (in too deep.) It's been two years; I miss my home, but there's a fire burn - in' in my bones. I

G | D |

still be - lieve, yeah, I still be - lieve. And all of these

⊕ Coda

C | Em | C | G |

I've still got a lot of fight left in me, a lot of fight left in me.

Verse 3

D | G | |

Like a small boat on the o - cean send-ing big waves

G | Em | C |

in-to mo - tion. Like how a sin-gle word can make a heart o - pen, I might on-ly have

G | |

one match that I can make an ex - plo - sion. This is my

Chorus

G | D | Em | C |

fight song, take back my life song, prove I'm al - right song. My pow - er's

G | D | Em |

turned on. Start-ing right now I'll be strong. I'll play my fight song. And I

C | G | D |

don't real-ly care if no - bod - y else be - lieves 'cause I've still got a lot of fight left in

Em | C | G ‖

me. No, I've still got a lot of fight left in me.

61

Don't You (Forget About Me)
featured in the Universal Picture THE BREAKFAST CLUB
Performed by Simple Minds
Arranged by NYC Guitar School

Word and Music by
Keith Forsey and Steve Schiff

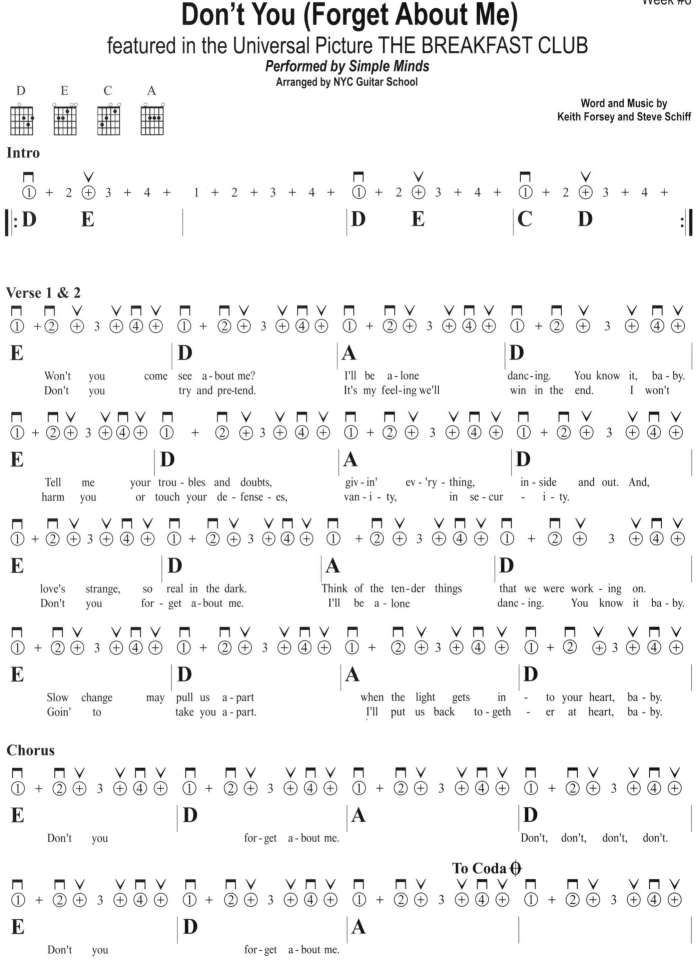

|: C | | | G | |

Will you stand a-bove me, look my way, nev-er love me?
Will you rec-og-nize me, call my name, or walk on by?

1. 2. **D.C. al Coda (take repeat)**

D | | A | | :|

Rain keeps fall-ing, rain keeps fall-ing down, down, down. down, down.

Bridge

|: D | E | D | A :|

But you walk on by. Will you call my name
as you walk on by? Will you call my name

|: D | E | D | A :|

when you walk a-way,
or will you walk a-way?

D | E | D |

Will you walk on by?

A | D | E |

Come on, call my name. Will you call my

D | A | D |

name? I say,

Outro   **Repeat and fade**

|: E | D | A | D :|

la, la, la, la, la, la, la, la, la, la, la, la, la, la, la, la.

Capo II

Mad World

Performed by Tears for Fears
Arranged by NYC Guitar School

Words and Music by
Roland Orzabal

Em   G   D   A

Intro

⊓ + 2 ⊕ 3 + 4 +   ⊓ + ② ⊕ 3 ⊕ ④ ⊕   ⊓ + ② ⊕ 3 ⊕ ④ ⊕   ⊓ + ② ⊕ 3 ⊕ ④ ⊕

Em

Verse 1

⊓ + ② ⊕ 3 ⊕ ④ ⊕   ⊓ + ② ⊕ 3 ⊕ ④ ⊕   ⊓ + ② ⊕ 3 ⊕ ④ ⊕   ⊓ + ② ⊕ 3 ⊕ ④ ⊕

‖: **Em** | **G** | **D** | **A** |

All a - round me are fa - mil - iar fac - es,   worn out plac - es,   worn out fac - es.
Their tears are fill - ing up their glass - es,   no ex - pres - sion,   no ex - pres - sion.

⊓ + ② ⊕ 3 ⊕ ④ ⊕   ⊓ + ② ⊕ 3 ⊕ ④ ⊕   ⊓ + ② ⊕ 3 ⊕ ④ ⊕   ⊓ + ② ⊕ 3 ⊕ ④ ⊕

Em | **G** | **D** | **A** :‖

Bright and ear - ly for their dai - ly rac - es,   go - ing no - where,   go - ing no - where.
Hide my head, I want to drown my sor - row,   no to - mor - row,   no to - mor - row.

Chorus

① + ② ⊕ 3 ⊕ ④ ⊕   ① + ② ⊕ 3 ⊕ ④ ⊕

‖: **Em** | **A**

had.   And I find it kind - a fun - ny,   I find it kind - a
  I find it hard to tell you,   'cause I find it hard to
(3., 4.) mad   world,

① + ② ⊕ 3 ⊕ ④ ⊕   ① + ② ⊕ 3 ⊕ ④ ⊕

Em | **A**

sad   the dreams in which I'm dy - ing are the best I've ev - er
take. When peo - ple run in cir - cles, it's a ver - y, ver - y
mad world.

Play 4 times :‖

Verse 2

⊓ + ② ⊕ 3 ⊕ ④ ⊕   ⊓ + ② ⊕ 3 ⊕ ④ ⊕   ⊓ + ② ⊕ 3 ⊕ ④ ⊕   ⊓ + ② ⊕ 3 ⊕ ④ ⊕

‖: **Em** | **G** | **D** | **A** |

Chil - dren wait - ing for the day they feel good,   hap - py birth - day,   hap - py birth - day.
Went to school and I was ver - y ner - vous,   no one knew me,   know one knew me.

⊓ + ② ⊕ 3 ⊕ ④ ⊕   ⊓ + ② ⊕ 3 ⊕ ④ ⊕   ⊓ + ② ⊕ 3 ⊕④ ⊕   ⊓ + ② ⊕ 3 ⊕ ④ ⊕

Em | **G** | **D** | **A** :‖

And to feel the way that ev - 'ry child should.   Sit and lis - ten,   sit and lis - ten.
Hel - lo, teach - er, tell me what's my les - son.   Look right through me,   look right through me.

Chorus

|: Em | A |

And   I   find   it   kind - a   fun - ny,   I   find   it   kind - a
had.   I   find   it   hard   to   tell   you,   'cause I   find   it   hard   to
(3., 4.)   mad   world,

Em | A   Play 4 times   :|

sad   the   dreams   in   which   I'm   dy - ing   are   the   best   I've   ev - er
take.   When   peo - ple   run   in   cir - cles,   it's   a   ver - y,   ver - y
                       mad   world.

Instrumental

Em | G | D | A |

Em | G | D | A |

Chorus

|: Em | A |

And   I   find   it   kind - a   fun - ny,   I   find   it   kind - a
had   I   find   it   hard   to   tell   you,   'cause I   find   it   hard   to
                   mad   world,

Em | A   Play 3 times   :|

sad   the   dreams   in   which   I'm   dy - ing   are   the   best   I've   ev - er
take.   When   peo - ple   run   in   cir - cles,   it's   a   ver - y,   ver - y
                       mad   world.

Em | A | Em | A |

En - lar - ging your   world.   Mad   world.

No Rain

Performed by Blind Melon
Arranged by NYC Guitar School

Words and Music by
Blind Melon

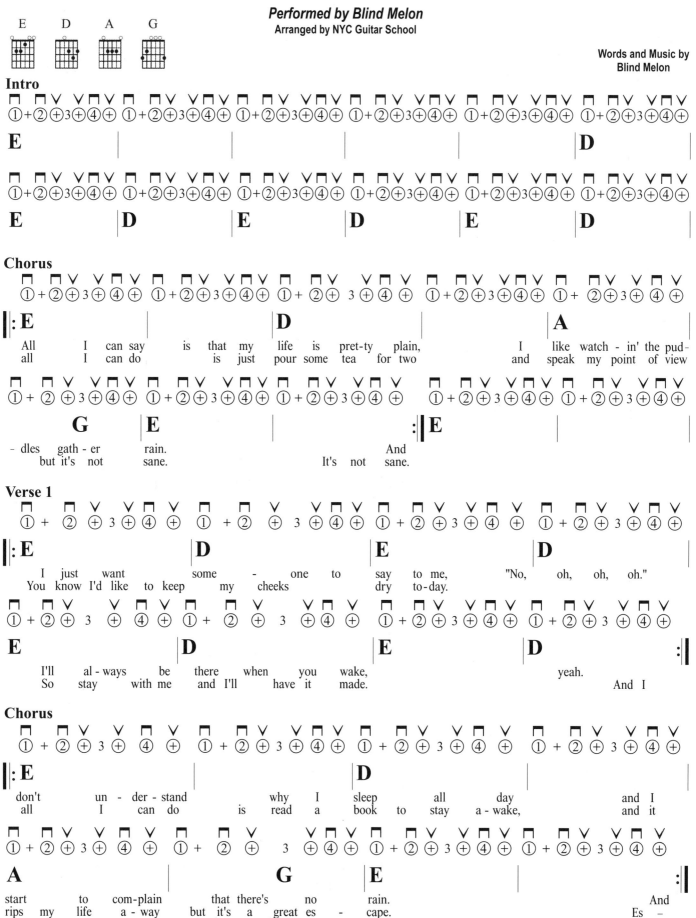

E

cape,   es - cape,   es - cape.

Instrumental

‖: E |D |E |D |

E |D |E |D   :‖

Chorus

E |D |

All   I   can say   is   that   my   life   is   pret-ty   plain,   you don't

A |G |E |

like   my   point of view,   you think that I'm in - sane.   It's   not

E | | | |

sane,   it's   not   sane.

Verse 2

‖: E |D |E |D |

I   just   want   some - one   to   say   to   me,   "No,   oh,   oh,   oh."
You know I'd like to keep   my   cheeks   dry   to-day.

E |D |E |D   :‖

I'll   al-ways   be   there   when   you   wake,   yeah.
So   stay   with me   and I'll   have it   made.

Outro

‖: E |D |E |D |

E |D |E |D   :‖

Come as You Are

Performed by Nirvana
Arranged by NYC Guitar School

Words and Music by
Kurt Cobain

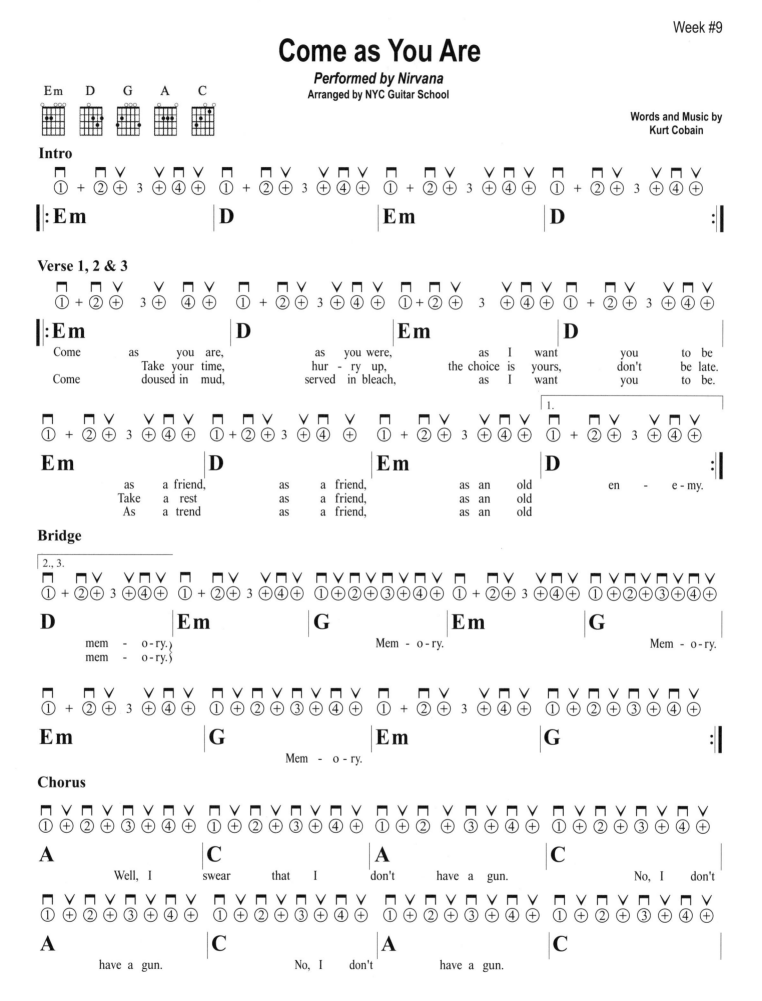

Interlude

① + ② + 3 + ④ + ① + ② + 3 + ④ + ① + ② + 3 + ④ + ① + ② + 3 + ④ +

Em | **D** | **Em** | **D** |

Solo

1.,-4.

① + ② + 3 + ④ + ① + ② + 3 + ④ + ① + ② + 3 + ④ + ① + ② + 3 + ④ +

‖: **Em** | **D** | **Em** | **D** :‖

Bridge

① + ② + 3 + ④ + ① + ② + ③ + ④ + ① + ② + 3 + ④ + ① + ② + ③ + ④ +

Em | **G** | **Em** | **G** |

Mem - o - ry.   Mem - o - ry.

① + ② + 3 + ④ + ① + ② + ③ + ④ + ① + ② + 3 + ④ + ① + ② + ③ + ④ +

Em | **G** | **Em** | **G** |

Mem - o - ry.

Chorus

① + ② + ③ + ④ + ① + ② + ③ + ④ + ① + ② + ③ + ④ + ① + ② + ③ + ④ +

A | **C** | **A** | **C** |

Well, I   swear   that   I   don't   have a gun.   No, I   don't

1.

① + ② + ③ + ④ + ① + ② + ③ + ④ + ① + ② + ③ + ④ + ① + ② + ③ + ④ +

‖: **A** | **C** | **A** | **C** :‖

have a gun.   No, I   don't   have a gun.   No, I   don't

Outro

2.

① + ② + 3 + ④ + ① + ② + 3 + ④ + ① + ② + 3 + ④ + ① + ② + 3 + ④ + ① + ② + 3 + ④ +

C | **Em** | **D** | **Em** | **D** |

Mem - o - ry.

① + ② + 3 + ④ + ① + ② + 3 + ④ + ① + ② + 3 + ④ + ① + ② + 3 + ④ + ① + 2 + 3 + 4 +

Em | **D** | **Em** | **D** | **Em** ‖

Mem - o - ry.

69

Despacito

Performed by Luis Fonsi
Arranged by NYC Guitar School

**Words and Music by Luis Fonsi,
Erika Ender, Justin Bieber,
Jason Boyd, Marty James Garton,
and Ramón Ayala**

Em   C   G   D

Verse 1 & 2

① + ② + 3 + ④ + ① + ② + ③ + ④ + ① + ② + 3 + ④ + ① + ② + ③ + ④ +

||: **Em** | | **C** |

Come on o - ver in my di - rec - tion. So thank-ful for that, it's such a bless - in',
You fit me, tail-or-made love, how you put it on. Got the on - ly key, know how to turn it on.

① + ② + 3 + ④ + ① + ② + ③ + ④ + ① + ② + 3 + ④ + ① + ② + ③ + ④ +

G | **D** |

yeah. Turn ev - 'ry sit - u - a - tion in - to heav - en, yeah. Oh, oh, you are
The way you nib-ble on my ear, the on-ly words I wan-na hear: Ba-by, take it slow so we can last long.

① + ② + 3 + ④ + ① + ② + ③ + ④ + ① + ② + 3 + ④ + ① + ② + ③ + ④ +

Em | | **C** |

my sun - rise on the dark - est day. Got me feel - in' some kind of
Tú, tú_e-res el i - mán y yo soy el me - tal. Me voy a - cer - can-do_y voy ar-man-do_el

① + ② + 3 + ④ + ① + ② + ③ + ④ + ① + ② + 3 + ④ + ① + ② + ③ + ④ +

G | **D** | :||

way. Make me wan - na sa - vor ev - 'ry mo - ment slow - ly, slow - ly.
plan. Só - lo con pen - sar - lo se_a - ce - ler - a_el pul - so. Oh, yeah.

① + ② + 3 + ④ + ① + ② + ③ + ④ + ① + ② + 3 + ④ + ① + ② + ③ + ④ +

Em | | **C** |

Ya, ya me_es - tá gus - tan-do más de lo nor - mal. To-dos mis sen - ti - dos va pi - dien - do más.

① + ② + 3 + ④ + ① + ② + ③ + ④ + ① + ② + 3 + ④ + ① + ② + ③ + ④ +

G | **D** |

Es-to_hay que to - mar - lo sin nin - gún a - pu - ro. Des - pa -

Chorus

Em | C |

ci - to. Quie - ro res - pi - rar tu cue - llo des - pa - ci - to. De - ja que te di - ga co-sas al o - i

G | D |

do, pa - ra que te_a - cuer - des si no_es-tás con-mi - go. Des - pa -

Em | C |

ci - to. Quei - so des-nu - dar-te_a be-sos des - pa - ei - to, fir-mo_en las pa - re-des de tu la - be-rin-

G | D |

- to, y_ha-cer de tu cuer-po to-do_un ma - scri - to.

Verse 3 & 6

Em | C |

Quie-ro ver bai-lar tu pe - lo, quei-ro ser tu rit - mo, que le_en-se-ñes a mi bo-

G | D |

- ca, tus lu - ga - res fa - vo - ri - tos.

Em | C |

Dé - ja-me so-bre-pa - sar - tus zo-nas de pe - li - gro, has - ta pro-vo-car tus gri-

To Coda

① + ② + 3 + ④ +   ① +   ② + ③ + ④ +   ① + ② + ③ + ④ +   ① + ② + ③ + ④ +

G | **D** |

- tos,   y que_ol - vi - des tu_a - pe - lli - do.   Si te pi - do_un be - so, ven

Verse 4

① + ② + 3 + ④ +   ① + ② + ③ + ④ +   ① + ② + 3 + ④ +   ① + ② + ③ + ④ +

Em | **C** |

dá - me - lo. Yo sé que_es - tás pen - sán - do - lo. Lle - vo tiem - po_in - ten - tán - do - lo, ma - mi_es - to_es dan - do_y dán - do - lo.   Sa - bes que tu

① + ② + 3 + ④ +   ① + ② + ③ + ④ +   ① + ② + ③ + ④ +   ① + ② + ③ + ④ +

G | **D** |

cor - a - zón con - mi - go te_ha - ce bang bang. Sa - bes que_e - sa be - ba_es - tá bus - can - do de mi bang bang. Ven prue - ba de mi

① + ② + 3 + ④ +   ① + ② + ③ +   ④ +   ① + ② + 3 + ④ +   ① + ② + ③ + ④ +

Em | **C** |

bo - ca pa - ra ver có - mo te sa - be.   Quie - ro, quie - ro quie - ro ver cuán - to a - mor a ti te ca - be.   Yo no ten - go

① + ② + 3 + ④ +   ① + ② + ③ + ④ +   ① + ② + ③ + ④ +   ① + ② + ③ + ④ +

G | **D** |

pri - sa, yo me quie - ro dar el via - je. Em - pe - ce - mos len - to, des - pués sal - va - je.   Pa - si - to_a pa -

Verse 5

① + ② + 3 + ④ +   ① + ② + ③ + ④ +   ① + ② + 3 + ④ +   ① + ② + ③ +   ④ +

Em | **C** |

si - to,   sua - ve sua - ve - ci - to.   Nos va - mos pe - gan - do po - qui - to_a po - qui - to   Y_es que_e - sa be -

D.S. al Coda

① + ② + 3 + ④ +   ① + ② + ③ +   ④ +   ① + ② + ③ + ④ +   ① + ② + ③ + ④ +

G | **D** |

lle - za_en un rom - pe - ca - be - zas, pe - ro pa'mon - tar - lo_a - qui ten - go la pie - za. ¡O - ye!

◐ Verse 7

① + ② ⊕ ③ + ④ ⊕ ① + ② ⊕ 3 ⊕ ④ ⊕ ① + ② ⊕ ③ + ④ ⊕

D   **|Em**

Des - pa - ci - to.   This is how we   do it down in   Puer - to Ri -

① + ② ⊕ ③ ⊕ ④ ⊕ ① + ② ⊕ ③ + ④ ⊕ ① + ② ⊕ 3 ⊕ ④ ⊕ ① + ② ⊕ ③ + ④ ⊕

C   **|**   **|G**

- co.   I just wan - na hear you scream-ing "¡Ay Ben - di - to!"   I can move for - ev - er se que-de con - ti -

① + ② ⊕ ③ ⊕ ④ ⊕ ① + ② ⊕ ③ + ④ ⊕ ① + ② ⊕ 3 ⊕ ④ ⊕ ① + ② ⊕ ③ + ④ ⊕

D   **|**   **|Em**

- go.   Pa - si - to_a pa - si - to,   sua-ve sua-ve - ci - to.   Nos va-mos pe -

① + ② ⊕ ③ ⊕ ④ ⊕ ① + ② ⊕ ③ + ④ ⊕ ① + ② ⊕ 3 ⊕ ④ ⊕ ① + ② ⊕ ③ + ④ ⊕

C   **|**   **|G**

gan - do po - qui - to_a pa - qui - to.   Y que_ol - vi - des tu_a - pe - lli - do.
Has - ta pro - vo - car tus   gri - tos.

① + ② ⊕ ③ ⊕ ④ ⊕ ① + ② ⊕ ③ + ④ ⊕

D

Des - pa - ci - to.

Let It Go

Performed by James Bay
Arranged by NYC Guitar School

Words and Music by
James Bay and Paul Barry

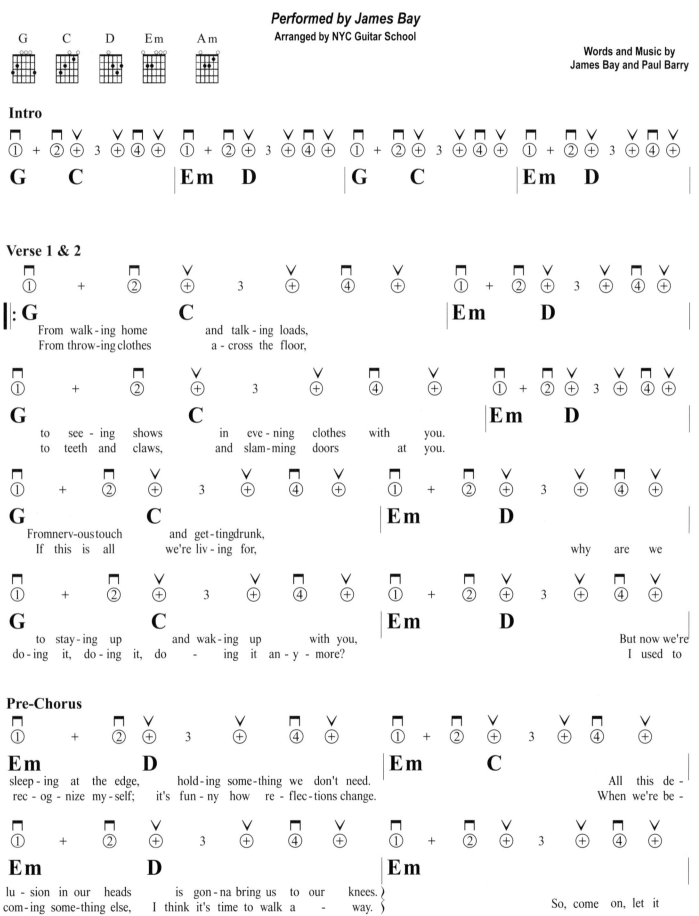

Chorus

C   G | Em   D
go,   just let it   be.   Why don't you be

Am   G | D
you   and I'll   be me?   Ev-'ry-thing that's

C   G | Em   D
broke   leave it   to   the   breeze.   Why don't you be

Am   G | D
you   and I'll   be me,   and I'll   be me?

Interlude

G   C | Em   D   G   C | Em   D   :||

Pre-Chorus

||:Am | G
   Try-'n' to fit your hand in-side of mine   when we know it just don't be-long.
   Try'n to push this prob-lem up the hill   when it's just too heav-y to hold.

D | Em   :||
There's   no force   on earth   could make it feel   right,   no.   Whoa.
I think   now's   the time   to   let   it   slide.   So come on, let it

Chorus

C   G |Em   D

go,   just   let   it   be.   Why   don't   you   be

C   G |D

you   and   I'll   be   me?   Ev-'ry - thing   that's

C   G |Em   D

broke   leave   it   to   the   breeze.   Let   the   ash - es

C   G |D

fall;   for - get   a - bout   be   me,   Come   on,   let   it

C   G |Em   D

go,   just   let   it   be.   Why   don't   you   be

Am   G |D

you   and   I'll   be   me,   and   I'll   be   me?

Outro

G   C |Em   D

G   C |Em   D |G

Man on the Moon

Performed by R.E.M.
Arranged by NYC Guitar School

Words and Music by William Berry,
Peter Buck, Michael Mills, and
Michael Stipe

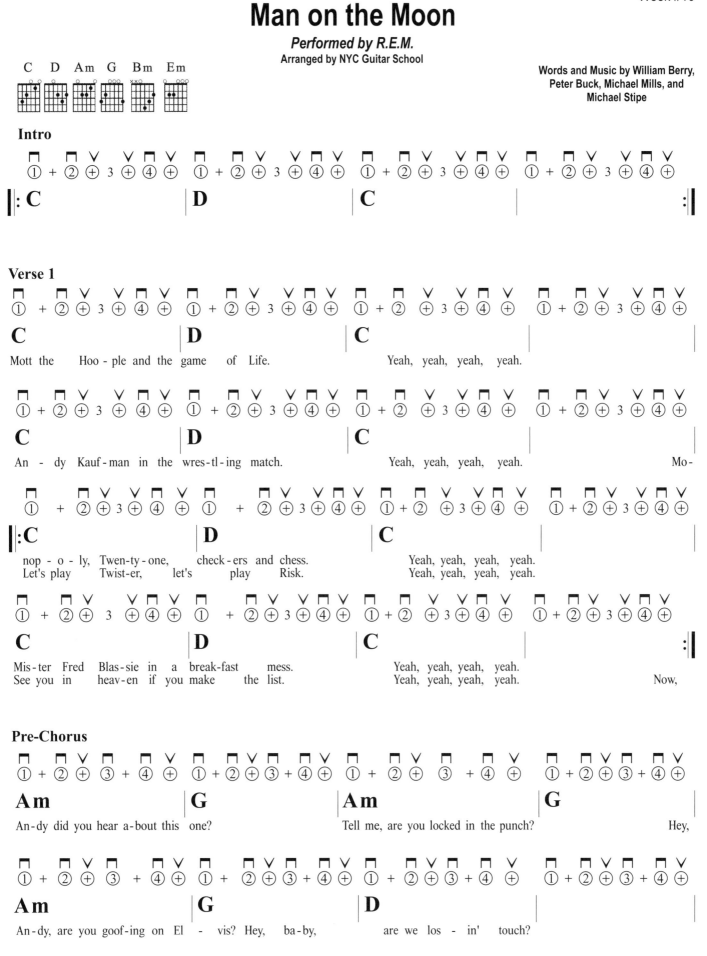

Chorus

G   Am |C   Bm |G   Am |D

If you be - lieved   they put a man on the moon,   man on the moon.

G   Am |C   Bm |Am

If you be - lieve   there's noth-ing up his sleeve,   then noth-ing is cool.

Verse 2

C |D |C

Mos-es went walk - ing with the staff of   wood.   Yeah, yeah, yeah, yeah.

C |D |C

New-ton got   beaned by the ap-ple   good.   Yeah, yeah yeah, yeah.

C |D |C

E - gypt was trou - bled by the hor-ri-ble asp.   Yeah, yeah, yeah, yeah.

C |D |C

Mis-ter Charles Dar-win had the gall   to ask.   Yeah, yeah, yeah, yeah.   Now,

Pre-Chorus

Am |G |Am |G

An-dy did you hear a-bout this one?   Tell me, are you locked in the punch?   Hey,

Am |G |D

An-dy, are you goof-ing on El - vis? Hey, ba-by,   are you hav - ing fun?

Chorus

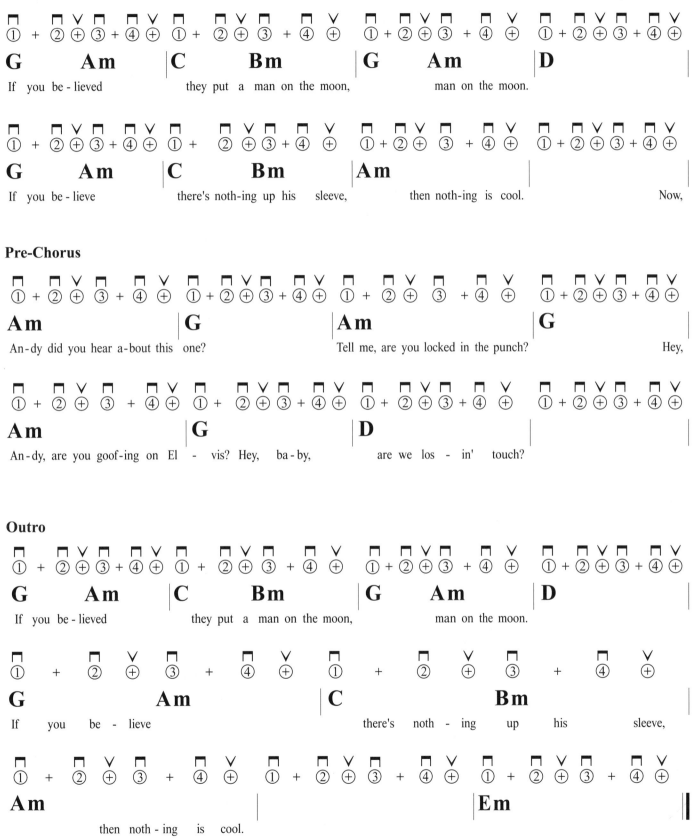

| G | Am | C | Bm | G | Am | D |

If you be - lieved they put a man on the moon, man on the moon.

| G | Am | C | Bm | Am |

If you be - lieve there's noth-ing up his sleeve, then noth-ing is cool. Now,

Pre-Chorus

| Am | G | Am | G |

An-dy did you hear a-bout this one? Tell me, are you locked in the punch? Hey,

| Am | G | D |

An-dy, are you goof-ing on El - vis? Hey, ba-by, are we los - in' touch?

Outro

| G | Am | C | Bm | G | Am | D |

If you be - lieved they put a man on the moon, man on the moon.

| G | Am | C | Bm |

If you be - lieve there's noth - ing up his sleeve,

| Am | Em |

then noth - ing is cool.

Tune down 1/2 step:
(low to high) Eb-Ab-Db-Gb-Bb-Eb
or Capo XI

My Name Is Jonas

Performed by Weezer
Arranged by NYC Guitar School

Words and Music by Rivers Cuomo,
Patrick Wilson and Jason Cropper

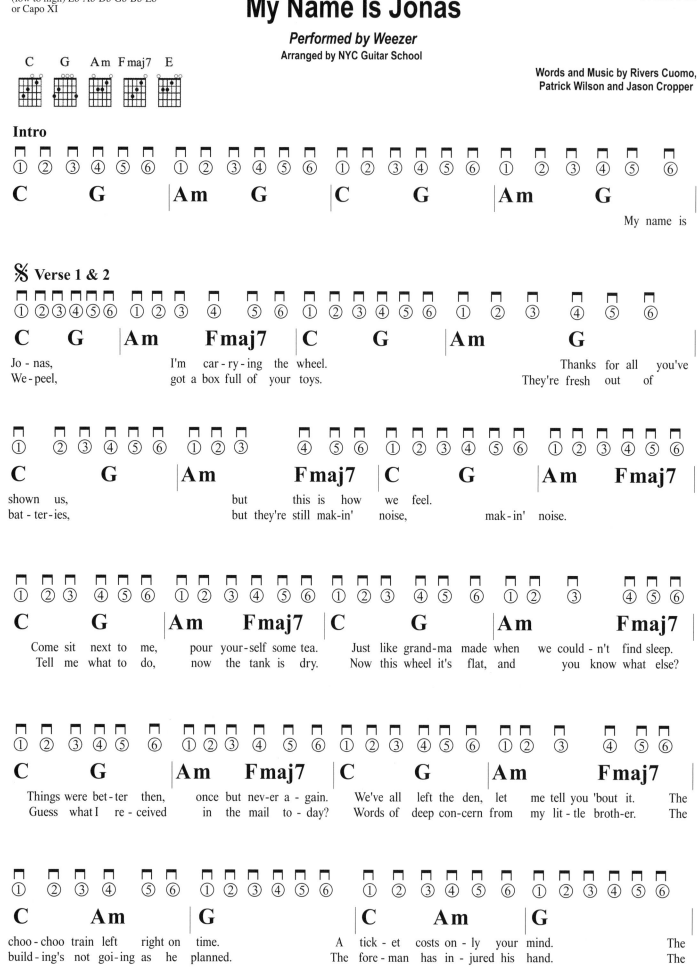

To Coda ⊕

① ② ③ ④ ⑤ ⑥ ① ②③④⑤⑥ ① ② ③ ④ ⑤ ⑥ ① ② ③ ④ ⑤ ⑥

C   **Am** |**G** |**C**   **Am** |**G** |

driv - er said, "Hey man, we go all the way."   Of course we were will - ing to pay.

doz - er will not clear a path.   The driv - er swears he learned his math.   The

Interlude   **D.S. al Coda**

① ② ③ ④ ⑤ ⑥ ① ② ③ ④ ⑤ ⑥ ① ② ③ ④ ⑤ ⑥ ① ② ③ ④ ⑤ ⑥

C   **G** |**Am**   **G** |**C**   **G** |**Am**   **G** |

My name is

⊕ **Chorus**

① ② ③ ④ ⑤ ⑥ ① ② ③ ④ ⑤ ⑥ ① ② ③ ④ ⑤ ⑥ ① ② ③ ④ ⑤ ⑥

Fmaj7 |**G** |**Fmaj7** |**G** |

work - ers are go - ing home,   work - ers are go - ing home.   The

① ② ③ ④ ⑤ ⑥ ① ② ③ ④ ⑤ ⑥ ① ② ③ ④ ⑤ ⑥ ① ② ③ ④ ⑤ ⑥

Fmaj7 |**G** |**Fmaj7** |**G** |

work - ers are go - ing home.   The work - ers are go - ing home.

Interlude

① ② ③ ④ ⑤ ⑥ ① ② ③ ④ ⑤ ⑥ ① ② ③ ④ ⑤ ⑥ ① ② ③ ④ ⑤ ⑥

C | | | |

Yeah!

① ② ③ ④ ⑤ ⑥ ① ② ③ ④ ⑤ ⑥ ① ② ③ ④ ⑤ ⑥ ① ② ③ ④ ⑤ ⑥

C   **Am** |**G** |**C**   **Am** |**G** |

① ② ③ ④ ⑤ ⑥ ① ② ③ ④ ⑤ ⑥ ① ② ③ ④ ⑤ ⑥ ① ② ③ ④ ⑤ ⑥

C   **Am** |**G** |**C**   **Am** |**G** |

The

E   Fmaj7 |G | E   Fmaj7 |G

work - ers are go - ing home. The work - ers are go - ing home. The

E   Fmaj7 |G | E   Fmaj7 |G |

work - ers are go - ing home. yeah, yeah, yeah.

Harmonica Solo

C   Am |G | C   Am |G

C   Am |G | C   Am |G

Outro

E   Fmaj7 |G | E   Fmaj7 |

G | | |C   G |

Am   G |C   G |Am   G |C |

My name is Jo - nas.

Sweet Child o' Mine

Performed by Guns N' Roses
Arranged by NYC Guitar School

Words and Music by W. Axl Rose, Slash,
Izzy Stradlin', Duff McKagan, and Steven Adler

D C G A

Em B7 E

Intro

‖: D | | C |

G | | D | :‖

℅ Verse 1 & 2

D

She's got a smile that it seems to me re - minds
She's got eyes of the blu - est skies As

C

if me of child - hood mem - o - ries, where ev -
if they thought of rain. I'd

G

– – 'ry - thing was as fresh as the bright blue sky.
hate to look in - to those eyes and

D

see an ounce of pain. Her

D

Now and then when I see her face she
hair re - minds me of a warm safe place where

□ ① + □ ② ∨ ⊕ 3 ∨ ⊕ □ ④ ∨ ⊕ □ ① + □ ② ∨ ⊕ 3 ∨ ⊕ □ ④ ∨ ⊕

C

takes me a - way to that spe - cial place, and if I
as a child I'd hide, and

□ ① + □ ② ∨ ⊕ 3 ∨ ⊕ □ ④ ∨ ⊕ □ ① + □ ② ∨ ⊕ 3 ∨ ⊕ □ ④ ∨ ⊕

G

stared too long, I'll prob - 'ly break down and cry.
pray for the thun - der and the rain to

□ ① + □ ② ∨ ⊕ 3 ∨ ⊕ □ ④ ∨ ⊕ □ ① + □ ② ∨ ⊕ 3 ∨ ⊕ □ ④ ∨ ⊕

D

qui - et - ly pass me by.

Chorus

□ ① + □ ② ∨ ⊕ 3 ∨ ⊕ □ ④ ∨ ⊕ □ ① + □ ② ∨ ⊕ 3 ∨ ⊕ □ ④ ∨ ⊕ □ ① + □ ② ∨ ⊕ 3 ∨ ⊕ □ ④ ∨ ⊕ □ ① + □ ② ∨ ⊕ 3 ∨ ⊕ □ ④ ∨ ⊕

A   **C**   **D**

Whoa, whoa, whoa, sweet child o' mine.

To Coda ⊕

□ ① + □ ② ∨ ⊕ 3 ∨ ⊕ □ ④ ∨ ⊕ □ ① + □ ② ∨ ⊕ 3 ∨ ⊕ □ ④ ∨ ⊕ □ ① + □ ② ∨ ⊕ 3 ∨ ⊕ □ ④ ∨ ⊕ □ ① + □ ② ∨ ⊕ 3 ∨ ⊕ □ ④ ∨ ⊕

A   **C**   **D**

Whoa, oh, oh, oh, sweet love o' mine.

Interlude

□ ① + □ ② ∨ ⊕ 3 ∨ ⊕ □ ④ ∨ ⊕ □ ① + □ ② ∨ ⊕ 3 ∨ ⊕ □ ④ ∨ ⊕ □ ① + □ ② ∨ ⊕ 3 ∨ ⊕ □ ④ ∨ ⊕ □ ① + □ ② ∨ ⊕ 3 ∨ ⊕ □ ④ ∨ ⊕

D   **C**

D.S. al Coda

□ ① + □ ② ∨ ⊕ 3 ∨ ⊕ □ ④ ∨ ⊕ □ ① + □ ② ∨ ⊕ 3 ∨ ⊕ □ ④ ∨ ⊕ □ ① + □ ② ∨ ⊕ 3 ∨ ⊕ □ ④ ∨ ⊕ □ ① + □ ② ∨ ⊕ 3 ∨ ⊕ □ ④ ∨ ⊕

G   **D**

D |A |C |D |

Oh, oh, oh, oh, sweet child o' mine. Oo, yeah, yeah!

A |C |D |

Oo, sweet love o' mine.

Guitar Solo

||: Em |C |B7 |Am **Play 3 Times** :||

Em |C |B7 |Am |

||: E |G |A |C D G |

E |G |A |C D G :||

Outro

||: E |G |A |C D G :||

YOUR ABSOLUTE BEGINNERS CHORD DICTIONARY

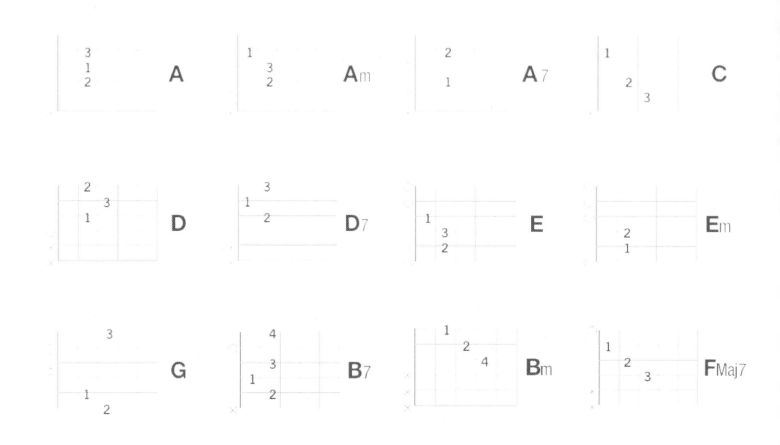

YOUR ABSOLUTE BEGINNERS STRUM LIBRARY